How To Build A (Semi) Solid Wall Yurt

by

Robert F. Lee

Published by Createspace for Robert F. Lee

Copyright 2013 Robert F. Lee

TABLE OF CONTENTS

INTRODUCTION — 4

CONSTRUCTION — 6

A. Floor — 6

B. Top and Bottom Plates — 13

C. Walls — 15

D. Windows — 19

E. Door — 20

F. Assembling & Erecting The Walls — 20

Door Segment — 26

Finishing the walls — 28

G. Roof — 29

H. The Rafter Ring — 32
    Installing the yurt rafter ring. — 34
    Installing roof insulation — 39

I. The Dome Vent — 40
    Raising the yurt dome vent — 45
    Installing the tarpaulin skins — 45
    Installing the aircraft cable. — 48
    Interior Finish — 49
    Building washrooms — 50

Plumbing & Responsible Water Use — 52

Lighting — 55

Heating — 59

Yurt Flooring — 60

Perimeter drainage 62

TIPS & ISSUES   64

Additional Problems & General Concerns 79

Interior Accessories 82

Build A Yurt Rafter Ring, Version Two 84

Disclaimer: engineers, permits, fire safety 86

Introduction

While many yurt packages are sold without flooring or insulation and most are sold without electrical or plumbing infrastructure, a permanent yurt requires all of these features to be considered complete.

The most popular type of yurt is the flexible wall system, which utilizes latticework in the interior as the form for the circular design. While these have great rustic appeal, they have inherent disadvantages – in fact, more disadvantages than advantages. On the other hand, solid-wall yurts become more like round, fixed-in-position houses than the in-touch-with-nature concept that drives their popularity. What works best is a hybrid of the two – a semi-solid design that provides structural integrity while offering close contact with nature and retaining the portability essence of any yurt.

One of the prevalent complaints about flexible wall yurts is the poor protection they provide against rodents, and animals such as raccoons, badgers and even bears or coyotes when the buildings are unoccupied. Bears, while reluctant to force their way through an apparently solid wall, are attracted by odours, and, in the late fall or early spring, may be sufficiently ravenous to attempt to claw their ways through the tent-like tarpaulins. Raccoons, unfortunately, pose chronic problems, and, being habituated to human contact, do not hesitate to slash their way through flimsy polyethylene or plastic coverings.

In cold climates, conventional foil-faced bubble insulation provides less than adequate insulation on its own – even when that foil-like material is space-age mylar. The high-tech insulation used in the space industry - mylar - is a costly option, but only moderately more effective, since it is not sold in the multi-layer structure required to be a good insulator. Fiberglass or cellulose batt insulation is a poor option when yurt walls are less than 3 ½ inches thick, and harbour flies in hot summer months. Consider that, in a yurt, you need to be concerned both with the cold and the hot, since there is no "attic" to dissipate radiant heat in summer, and, in winter, thin walls mean reduced volume of insulation materials.

This guide will take you, step by step, through the construction of a simple sixteen-foot diameter semi-solid wall yurt, with sufficient data to enable you to easily scale your yurt larger or smaller. Indeed, my first yurt, using many of the constructs in this new design, was built as a twenty-eight foot diameter structure. It easily survived throughout the four Manitoba winters that I owned it, where temperatures dipped to minus 46 degrees. The summers saw some of the wettest and windiest conditions that the province had endured, yet the yurt stood without fail.

An option for yurt living is to construct two or more smaller yurts, joined together by a breezeway, rather than a wider yurt requiring additional structural support for the roof assembly. This allows for maximum airflow around the units, expansion as desired, and simplicity of construction.

In sections following the construction and assembly phases, you will encounter discussions on various issues and options that we explored, when we built and moved into our first yurt.

At the end of this guide, you will find photos, drawings and figures that illustrate the construction, assembly and disassembly process for your yurt. Ideally, you should be able to assemble your yurt kit in less than three hours and take it down in less than two hours. With dedicated effort, you should be able to build the package in less than seven days. And you should be able to build your prototype for under $2,500. Not bad for a camper, cabin and summer home substitute!

Construction

A. Floor

The floor, like the rest of this yurt, is designed to be lightweight, portable, easily assembled and disassembled, inexpensive and durable. These may seem difficult standards to reconcile, but are surprisingly simple. Materials consist of high density rigid foam insulation or polystyrene, 2 by 2s, one-by-six lengths of spruce, pine or fir, one-by-three lengths of SPF, 7/16 (or ½) OSB or plywood and a small quantity of 2", 2 ½" and 3" deck screws, as well as a few pieces of scrap wood for levelling the floor on uneven surfaces.
Begin by cutting seven lengths of eight-foot 1*6 into 94.5 inches for each of the eight-foot by eight-foot sections of the 16 by 16 foot yurt platform. If you are planning on including a deck in the design, allow for two more sections of platform. Mark along the face of each 1*6 the depth of the rigid insulation that you will be using. (Minimum recommended thickness is 1.5").
Next, cut twelve pieces of one-by-three to 94.5 inch lengths per platform section.
Using wood or carpenter's glue, apply a liberal amount of adhesive to one side of a one-by-three, then align the one-by-three top edge with the marks on each one-by-six, with the glue edge toward the 1*6 and clamp together. Using the 2" screws, join the two pieces, placing screws offset from each other at one-foot intervals. Each 8*8 section will require two of these joined sets.

Using the same process, attach one-by-threes to each side of a one-by-six. You will require five of these sets per eight-foot section of platform.

(Note that the use of 1 by 6 joined floor joists is intended to provide the most lightweight option for your portable yurt floor. If you are unconcerned about weight and portability, substitute this assembly for 2*6 joists, with 1.5" (or 2", depending upon thickness of your rigid insulation) deep by 0.5" wide notches on either side of the joist, allowing the insulation to rest in these channels upon completion)
Next, cut one 1*6 into four lengths of 14.5 inches and two lengths of 13.75 inches (per platform section). Cut each of these pieces into 2 ¾ inch widths.
Mark two 1*6s at 16" intervals. Lay out and temporarily screw together the assembled 1*6/1*3 combinations to each of the marked 1*6s, so that the 1*6 parts of the combinations are centred on the 16" marks, forming a framework of seven joists and two 1*6 headers. Make sure that the 1*6/1*2 combinations with only one 1*6 each are used at either end, with the 1*6 attachments facing toward the other joists.

Using the first 13.75 piece of 1 by 2 ¾, fasten it on the inside of the 1*6 marked header, between the first and second 1*6/1*3 combination joist with three 2" screws and wood glue, aligning the top of the 2 ¾ inch width with the top of each adjacent 1 by 3 strip. This piece should fit tightly between these segments. Do the same between the two joists at the opposite end of the section, and repeat on the other header. Using each of the 14.5 inch pieces, screw them in place between each of the remaining joists. All pieces should fit snugly in place. If they do not, re-measure and realign the spaces between the joists, keeping in mind that the 4by 8 foot sheet of OSB that will be used later as a subfloor must align precisely along the centre of the 1*6 joist.

Cut two 2*2s into four lengths of 14.5 inches and two lengths of 13.75 inches per board (per platform section). Aligning the 2*2 top edge with the top edge of the 1*3 part of the 1*6/1*3 combination, fit one of these pieces between the joists at the 2.5 foot distance from each header. This will provide additional support for the rigid insulation that will rest in the channels created by the joist assemblies.

Cut four pieces of 2*2 into 20.5 inch lengths, with 45 degree end cuts. Toenail one end of the first piece to the third joist where the cross brace 2*2 meets the joist, and the other end along the adjacent fourth joist. Fasten the second piece in the same manner between the fourth and fifth joist. Fasten the third piece between the second and third joists on the opposite end, and the fourth between the fifth and sixth joist. These braces provide diagonal support while you complete the assembly, and help to support the rigid insulation.

Assemble each 8 by 8 foot section of the floor individually and then join the four pieces together to form a larger, 16 by 16 square. Be sure that the pieces are level with each other, and join using screws spaced approximately eighteen inches apart. Level the floor section, placing support blocks wherever needed to provide a solid surface on which the joists rest.

Cut the 1.5 inch rigid insulation into four pieces measuring 14.5 inches wide by 94.5 inches long. Cut two pieces of rigid insulation measuring 13.75" by 94.5". Fit each of these pieces into the cavities between the joists, using the narrow 13.75" pieces on each end.

Now take the first sheet of OSB or plywood, and lay it along the outer edge of one of the sections, making sure that it lines up with the outer edge of the outside joist or header and the at the centre line along the joist that is 4 feet into the section. Lay the second sheet on the next floor segment, so that the four-foot width of the first sheet is aligned with the four-foot width of the second sheet, and that this second sheet lines up along the outside edge of the outer joist and second header. Be sure that, like the first sheet, the inner edge lines up along the centre of the four-foot joist.

Place the next four sheets perpendicular to these two sheets, making sure that one edge on each sheet falls along the centre line of the four-foot joist on the first (and second) segment, and the other end falls along the centre of the four-foot joist of the next segment to it. Place the last two sheets on the far end of the last two segments, so that they are aligned parallel to the first two and perpendicular to the other four. By laying out the sheets in this manner, you will ensure that the four floor segments are tied securely together. Fasten the sheets in place using 2" screws spaced sixteen inches apart along each joist and header.

Your floor deck is complete, and may be finished using indoor/outdoor carpet loosely laid on top.

Time to cut and assemble floor: 1.5-2.0 hours per 8*8 platform section.
Materials (for 4 8' by 8' sections):
1" by 6", 8' length – 36
1" by 3", 8' length – 48
(or substitute above two items for 36 2" by 6", 8' lengths)
2" screws – 2.5 lb.
1.5" thick rigid insulation, 4' by 8' – 8
Wood glue – 1 pint
7/16 OSB, 4' by 8' sheets – 8
2" by 2", 8' lengths - 6

B. Top and Bottom Plates

The key to the structural integrity of these walls is the uniquely designed top and bottom plate collection. You will require forty-seven of these plates (one is not needed at the base of the door segment).

To construct the pieces, I recommend using two by eight dimensional lumber. Cut three eight-foot lengths into twenty-four inch pieces (48 in all. One quarter of the plates will have a slightly narrowed end that does not impact on strength. These can be used in the bottom plate assembly.)

Mark the twelve inch point midway along the top and bottom edges of the length of each piece. Next, mark 1.6 inches down from the top edge on each of the ends of the board. Draw lines from the centred 12 inch top mark to each of the 1.6 inch marks, creating a shallow "vee" appearance. Draw a vertical line between the two twelve inch marks. Mark points 1.5, 3.0, 4.5 and 6.0 inches from the top centre mark.

From the top edge (corner) on each end, measure down 3.1, 4.6 and 6.1 inches, marking these locations. Now draw lines, parallel to the first set of "vee" lines, connecting the 3.1 inch point and the centre 12 inch line at the 1.5 inch point. Repeat for the lines connecting the 3.0 and 4.6 inch and 4.5 and 6.1 points.

Using your steel square (it is 1.5 inches wide on the narrow edge) or using a strip of 2 by 4 laid on edge (a 2 by 4 is actually 1.5 inches by 3.5 inches), place the 1.5 inch width along the line that leads from the 3.0 to 4.6 inch points. The mark that you made at the 6.0 inch point on the centre line should coincide with the outer edge of the 1.5 inch width. Draw a line from the 4.5 inch point, along the 1.5 inch width, to a point that ends a short distance in along the bottom edge of the 2 by six.

Begin by cutting of the pieces from the 1.6 to 0 inch (top centre 12" point) with your table saw. Now, cut part way along each of the lines (about 2/3 of the distance to the centre line from the outer edge) that you have drawn from outer edge to centre line, using your circular saw. Do not cut all the way to the centre point, as, due to the design of the saw blade, the underside will have cut further along the line than you can observe at the top of the board. Once these cuts have been completed, use your jigsaw to cut the rest of the way to the centre line. This will create four "vee" shaped pieces of top and bottom plate per two-foot segment of two by six. Each piece will form a 15 degree angle, but the outer ends will have a 97.5 degree angle to them.

Lastly, use your mitre saw to cut the outer ends of each piece to 90 degree angles, without cutting any of the length off the outer edge of each arm. (Note that the outer arms will measure 12 inches, while the length between the centre crux of the "vee" and the far inside edge will be approximately 11.8 inches).

Time: 1.5 hours
Materials: (4) 2 by 8 – 8 feet long

C. Walls

The semi-solid walls are exceptionally easy to construct. They are built using two-foot wide panels. For the sixteen-foot (exact diameter is 15 feet 3.35 inches) wide yurt, you will need twenty-three of them. The height of the walls is up to you. However, we recommend that the wall units be at least seven feet high, as you will be using a standard eighty-one inch door for your entrance, and the upper cross member will be 1.5 inches deep. This sample yurt is built to eighty-four inches in height.
Each panel consists of two 22 3/8" long - 2" by 2" inch cross members or chords (not "plates," since they are built inside, not on top and bottom of the upright studs), one 22 3/8" by 69" length of rigid insulation, two seven-foot long one by two inch studs and one piece of polyethylene medium duty tarpaulin measuring 73 inches tall by 54.5 inches wide.
Begin by cutting your studs to the appropriate length (72 inches).

Set your table saw or mitre saw (or circular saw if your hands are steady) at a 7.2 degree angle (7 degrees is close enough). Marking your 2 by 2s to 22 3/8 inch lengths, cut the pieces so that each end is sloped inward at the 7.2 degree angle. Be sure that the two ends angle in toward each other. This angle cut is necessary so that each wall segment fits tightly into the arc of the circumference of the yurt. You may choose to cut the pieces at 90 degree angles, but you will need to allow approximately 3/8 inch for the gap that will be created between each segment during erection of the walls. This gap, while not desirable, is not critical, since you will be covering the entire outer walls with a second tarpaulin skin, and, if you are erecting the yurt as a permanent placement, you can fill the gap with spray foam insulation, packed fibreglass insulation or caulking. It will not be seen once the outer skin is installed.

Note that, if you are using Roxul semi-rigid cellulose-based insulation instead of rigid extruded polystyrene (closed or open cell), you may use a third 2*2 cross member, fastened at the 4-foot mark in each wall, for added rigidity.

Screw the cross members between the 1*2 studs, using 2.5 inch screws.

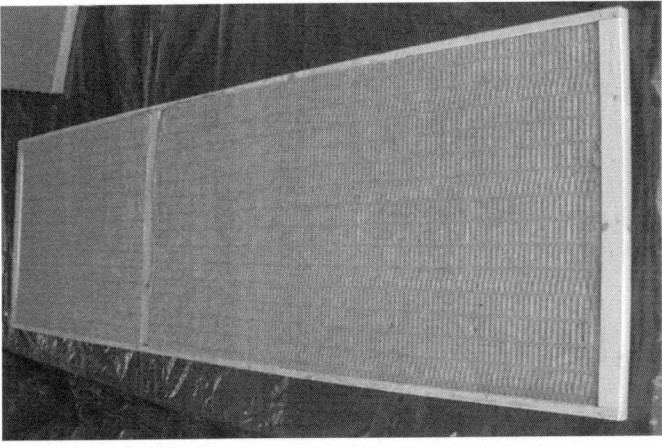

Cut the rigid insulation to 22 3/8 inches by 69 inches and slide into the gap between the studs from the wide side. The insulation will compact sufficiently to slide into place at the narrow portion.
Cut your tarpaulin to 75 inches by 54.5 inches.
Lay the structure on the tarpaulin with the height of the segment parallel to the 75-inch length. Allow for an overlap of 1.5 inches on the top and bottom, and 1.5 inches on the long edge. Staple the 1.5 inch overlap of the long edge to the 1*2 stud, making sure that it lines up evenly along the upper edge of the panel. Use one staple every eight inches.

Flip the panel to the other side, and, drawing the tarp tightly and evenly across the panel, staple this edge in the same manner as you did the first. Now, flip the panel again so that the first stapled edge is facing you, and run a thin bead of hot glue along this edge of the tarp that is stapled. Be careful not to apply too much glue, or to allow the gun to touch the fabric, as it will burn through the tarp quickly. Then, drawing the tarp tightly around the panel, bring the loose edge in line with the bottom lip of the long edge, pressing the tarp into the glue before it hardens, and stapling it into place. Make sure that the soft glue is pressed flat, so that there are no bulges or ridges of glue. Complete the wall panel by gluing and stapling the top and bottom edges of the tarpaulins to the cross members.

Time: 8-10 hours
Material list:
Medium duty tarpaulin, FR – 650-700 sq. ft. (71-77 sq. yd)
Dowels, 3/8" – 69
Package strapping – 50 ft.
Mini-glue sticks – 27
3/8 staples – 1,000 (1 pkg)
1.5 inch thick rigid insulation, 4' by 8' sheets – 12

2.5 inch screws – 3.5 lb.
2" by 2", 8' length – 14
1" by 2", 8' lengths - 46

D. Windows

For windows, use the same process for framing your wall segment. Do not affix the tarpaulin yet.
Since you will be using shed windows that are eighteen inches wide by 24 inches tall, you will need to cut two 34 ½ inch lengths of two by two and screw one to the left one-by-two stud, from the top edge of the bottom plate. Cut three additional 22 ¼ inch two by twos with the 7.2 degree angle that is identical to all other chords. Place one of the 22 3/8 inch chords on top of the jack stud between the two studs, level and secure into place using a 3" screw through the chord into the jack stud and one screw toenailed into each end to the 1*2 studs. Mark a distance of 16 ¾ inches, from the centre of the two by two jack stud on this chord. Place the second jack stud so that it is centred on the 22 3/8 mark and secure by screwing a 3" screw through this upper and bottom chords into the jack stud. Measuring from the top of the chord that you placed on the jack studs, mark a point on the long studs that is 24 ¼ inches from the top of the bottom window chord. Cut two 24 ¼ lengths of 2 by 2. Frame the window buck using the two lengths that you just cut and a 22 3/8 chord on top in the same way that you installed the two jack studs and window bottom chord. Place the window in the frame to ensure that it fits fairly snugly. Remove the window and fill the gaps with insulation.
Attach the tarpaulin wrap in the same manner that you did for the regular wall segments. Cut diagonally from the upper left inside corner of the window box to the lower right, and then from the upper right to the lower left on each side. Trim these triangular flaps so that there is a 1.5 inch strip of tarp remaining along each side. You will notice that there is a gap with no tarpaulin at each corner. This is not significant.

Run a bead of hot glue around the outside edge of the window frame and secure the tarpaulin in the normal manner. Staple and glue around the outer edge of the window box. Run glue around the inside lip of the window frame and fold over the tarp from the other side, pressing the tarp into place and stapling it. You may, if you choose, glue fragments of that tarp residue into the gaps at the window frame corners.

The window will not be installed at this time. However, you may wish to test that it still fits properly, since, if you have used too much glue, there may be ridges that make installing the window difficult. It is easier to remove excess glue while it is still warm, than it is to remove the excess later.

Time: 1.5 hours
Material list: 3 shed windows, 18" by 24"

E. Door

The door panel section uses two by four stud construction, instead of 1 by 2, because the door requires heavier structural support. This panel will be made separately from the other wall segments, and will allow us to adjust our dimensions to compensate for any minor errors in fabrication that may have occurred with the wall lengths.
Time: see below
Material list: see below

F. Assembling & Erecting The Walls

Window Location: When you lay out your yurt for the first time, you will be able to choose the layout and location of windows and doors. While this seems mundane, it is an important consideration that factors in prevailing wind direction in each season, sunlight and access.

Windows, in addition to providing light, also provide ventilation and cross-ventilation, as well as heat loss and gain. In the summer (which is when most portable yurt use occurs), heat gain is significant through windows. While the roof vent is an excellent means to dissipate that heat, you can minimize gain by orienting your windows to let in early morning and late afternoon sun, with minimal direct sunlight in the mid-afternoon. At the same time, you need cross-ventilation. This requires that windows not be placed too closely together, and that, if you are erecting interior walls (e.g. for washroom), that light and ventilation are not restricted. Ideally, the three windows and the door are placed in separate quadrants of the structure, to maximize air movement. However, if you are planning on using the yurt in colder seasons, ensure that the prevailing winds in those seasons (typically north, northwest) are not blowing directly on window area. Also, by locating windows so that one of the windows is always in shade (not necessarily the same one at all times!), you will increase natural air flow because of the temperature difference between sunlit and unlit windows.

The door location should be determined based on primary rain and snowfall direction. In most cases, doors should be oriented toward a blocking structure, such as another building, a stand of trees, etc., so that rain is not forced into the door during high winds.

Once you have chosen the locations of your openings, begin laying out the bottom plates in a perimeter on the circle that you have marked on your platform. To do this, beginning on the left side of the door segment and working clockwise (as if looking down from above the yurt), place the first bottom plate at the point where the door frame wall segment will be. Work around the circle, securing each bottom plate with one screw only (partly screwed in place), six inches to either side of the "vee" apex on each piece. This will allow you to adjust the position of each plate, if necessary. Do not worry about window placement at this time.

Verify that the entire platform is level. Because you are working in a circle, a slight variation from level will result in skewed measurements when the walls are installed, and will prevent you from aligning the segments vertically.

The final diameter of this yurt is slightly less than sixteen feet (15.27 feet). When you scribe the perimeter circle as a guide to laying out the bottom plates, ensure that you measure 7.64 feet as a radius from the centre point. The bottom plate outside edge will line up with this line.

As you lay out all the bottom plates, you will find that once all pieces are in place, you have a space between the first and the last that should be forty-eight inches, or slightly less. This is the space allotted for the specially constructed door wall segment, using two by four construction.

If you are satisfied that the bottom plates are properly fitted, tighten all screws in place.

Now mark the positions of the windows on the perimeter. Be sure that, when you are erecting the wall sections in place, that you put the segments containing the window openings here.

On each bottom plate, measure four inches from the point of the "vee" to either side. Mark a point on each arm of the bottom plate that is centred on the plate ¾ inch from either edge and four inches from the apex of the "vee." Drill 3/8 inch holes that are ¾ inch deep at these points. Apply a small amount of carpenter's glue to one end of a dowel, and insert it into the first hole halfway. Repeat for the second arm of the plate, and continue in like manner for each plate. Allow them to dry. These dowels will fit into the holes that you will drill in the bottom of each wall panel as you assemble the unit.

Begin by placing the first wall section at the left hand side of the door frame location, with the slope of the studs facing inward. Align the segment in position and mark the location of the two dowels in the bottom plates. Drill holes ¾ inch deep by 3/8 inch, so that the dowels in the bottom plate fit into the holes snugly.

On each one by two stud, mark a point exactly forty-two inches from the bottom of the stud and exactly ¾ inch from either edge of the 1 ½ inch width. Drill a 3/8 inch hole through each stud. Later, you will be inserting 1 ½ inch long wooden dowels in these holes to align the walls as they are erected.

Now that the glue has hardened, locate the hole that you drilled at the 42 inch mark of the right stud (as you look at the wall from the inside) and punch through the fabric using a sharp tool such as an awl, sharp punch or utility knife. Apply a small amount of carpenter's glue to one end of the 1 ½ inch dowel, and insert it into the hole halfway. Allow it to dry. This dowel will fit into the hole on the left side of the adjacent wall as you assemble the structure. (Note: be sure that you put only one dowel in each wall, and that it is installed in the right-hand stud as you look at the wall from the inside.)

Slide the first panel into place over the dowels in the bottom plates. Tap the wall segment into place from the top so that the bottom chord of the segment rests on the platform. Temporarily attach a brace to the front and back of the panel so that the panel is vertical. Align the first top plate on top of this panel so that the apex of the "vee" aligns with the outer edge of the segment and so that the outer edge length of the plate lines up along the length of the segment top chord. Secure the plate in place using two 3" screws placed about four inches apart on the first arm of the plate. Do not tighten the screws down at this time.

Prepare the second segment in the same manner as the first, drilling holes for the bottom dowels and for the dowels and holes placed at the 42" height on the studs.

When placing this and subsequent panels into position, make sure that the dowel in the side fits into its corresponding hole. Once you have levelled the panel so that it is flush with the first, and is vertical on all sides, insert two screws in the second arm of the top plate, through into the top chord of this wall segment. Tighten all four screws in the top plate.

Place a second top plate, in the same manner as the first, on top of the second panel top chord. The end of this plate should meet snugly against the end of the first plate. Secure it with two screws as you did with the first panel. Continue, erecting each panel and window wall segment in sequence. Make sure that each panel is level and vertical on all sides before proceeding to the next panel.

Door Segment

Once all of the remaining panels have been erected, measure the distance between last wall segment and the first . Cut two 2 by 4s to this length. Along their length, rip these boards into 2 ¾ inch by 1 ½ inch (by the cut length) pieces. (This is done so that the door frame, which is 81 inches, will fit comfortably into the frame and allow for adjustment.) Now cut four two by fours to 77 ¾ inches.

Lastly, measure the distance between the two bottom plates and subtract the exterior width of the door (including its built-in buck, or frame). Then subtract the width of the four two by four studs (6 inches). Divide that distance by two. (e.g. space between plates is 48". Door and buck is 33 1/2 inches. 2 by 4s are six inches. 48-33.5 = 14.5 inches. 14.5 – 6 = 8.5 inches. 8.5 inches / 2 = 4 ¼ inches.). Cut two pieces of 2 by 4 to that length.

To assemble this door wall segment, first splice together the two long top pieces that you first cut. Then toenail two of the studs to this spliced top plate, so that the top plate rests on the studs. Measure from the inside of each stud toward the centre point on the top plate a distance that is the same as the length of the two small pieces of 2 by 4 that you cut last. This mark will be the outside edge of the next two studs. Toenail them in place to the top plate. You will find that, with the structure laying flat on the ground, you can install these studs more accurately if you lay the two small pieces between the stud you are toe-nailing and the outside studs temporarily. This will ensure that the spacing is the same at the top and bottom of the door opening. Now, lay the first of the two small pieces between the two studs on one side of the opening, at the bottom and secure to the studs. Do the same for the remaining piece on the other side. Temporarily lay the door and buck assembly inside the opening and nail a temporary cross brace across the opening, so the frame is held in position during erection. (Do not, at this time, put the door wall segment into place in the yurt perimeter.

Slide the door assembly into place so that it fits snugly between the first and last wall segments, with the outer edges of the wall segments and the outer edges of the door frame aligning. Screw the bottom of the door assembly into place, and then level the door unit. Toenail (using 2.5" screws) from the door 2 by 4 frame into the adjacent wall 1 by 2s. The extended arms of the top plates on the first and last wall segments should rest tightly on the top 2 by 4 of the door frame. Secure the top plates to the top of the door frame using four 3" screws. Cut a piece of 2 by 2 that is the same length as the distance between the ends of the two top plates and screw it into place between the two plates, so that there is a continuous run of 2 by 2 top plate around the entire structure.

Time:1.75 hrs.
Materials:
32" wide door assembly – 1
2" by 4", 8' lengths – 5
Screws, 3" – ¼ lb

Finishing the walls

On each top plate, drill a 3/8 inch hole ¾ inch deep exactly ¾ inch from the outside of the apex of the "vee." Apply a small amount of carpenters glue to one end of a 1 ½ inch by 3/8 inch wooden dowel, and insert the dowel into the hole. This dowel will align with the holes that you will be drilling in the rafters later, and will allow for easy alignment of the rafters and support while assembling the unit. The space between dowels (centre to centre) should be 24".

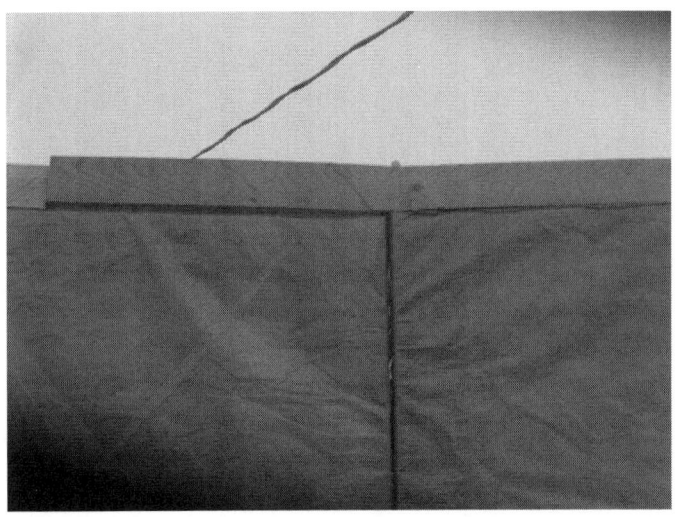

Wind endurance is significantly greater in a properly designed solid wall yurt, as well. Using the interlocking top and bottom plate segments that has been created for these units, the structures have endured winds of over 115kph, without any sign of stress or strain.

Time: 1.25 hr
Materials: previously listed

G. Roof

The roof structure, aside from the rafter ring, is extremely simple to construct and assemble. The rafters consist of twenty-five 2" by 4" by 8 foot pieces of dimensional SPF lumber.
To begin, use your mitre saw to cut a 30 degree angle on one end of each stud by laying the length of 2 by 4 along the parallel guide and setting the saw to 30 degrees.

Next, using a segment of plywood or OSB as a guide to establish a 90 degree angle (perpendicular) to the mitre saw back guide, by laying the plywood along the cut line when the mitre saw is set at 0 degrees. Now, swing the blade so that the mitre gauge is set to 30 degrees, and place the length of the 2 by 4 perpendicular to the back guide of the saw and along the edge of the piece of square plywood. Make sure that the finished cut will slope inward, on the same edge as the 60 degree cut and so that the two cuts angle toward each other.

If you do not have a mitre saw, the following method will allow you to make the same angle cut. Measure a 30 degree angle from the corner of the two by four so that when this rafter heel rests on the top plate of the wall, it will form a 30 degree rise toward the roof peak and so that the gouged channels will be to the top of the rafter, allowing the insulation to rest in the grooves. To do this, recall that the formula for the lengths of each side of a 30-60-90 triangle is 1-2-sqrt3. The simplest way (aside from using a guide set to 30 degrees on your saw!) is to measure 6 inches along the top long edge of the rafter. Then, using a pin tied to a string, measure a 3 inch length on the string. Pierce the pin into the six inch mark on the top edge of the rafter, and scribe an arc by holding a pencil at the 3" mark and the pin at the 6" point on that edge. Now measure 5.19 inches on the string and secure the pencil at that point. Pierce the pin into the bottom heel corner of the rafter and scribe a 5.19" arc on the board. At the point where the two arcs intersect, draw lines to the corner and to the upper 6" point. This is a 30-60-90 triangle. Cut out the material to conform to this dimension.

Cut a 60 degree angle on the opposite end, with the slope running toward the slope of the bottom heel 30 degree cut, and so that, when installed, the cut edge of the stud will be perpendicular to the floor. This upper heel will rest on the rafter ring.

Set your table saw blade to a 1 ½ depth, and the guide to 5/8 inch wide. With the two by four standing so that the 3 ½ (4") height is parallel to the ripping blade and the angles that you have cut are on the upper side of the board, cut a grove the entire eight foot length of the piece on the lower side. Now turn the board around lengthwise so that the groove is on the bottom again, but outside (away from) the blade, with the 3 ½ inch height vertical, and rip a second 1 ½ deep grove in the length of the board.

Set your blade to ½ inch deep and the guide to 1 ½ inches wide, and rip along the length of the board to remove the strip of waste material formed as the ½ inch cut meets the 1 ½ cut. Repeat the process for the other side and the 1 ½ by ½ inch channel.

These two channels will hold the rigid insulation in place once they are installed in place. Note that, if you have a dado blade, you can use this blade in one pass to make a ½ by 1 ½ gouge, instead of using two passes of the ripping blade.

Once you have completed the thirty and sixty degree cuts at either end of the rafters, trim exactly two inches from the end of the thirty degree cut, perpendicular to the hypotenuse (the heel portion) of the rafter. This will mean that, after the cut, there will be a thicker edge to the heel, providing additional strength to the rafter as it rides on the top plates.

Now, drill a 3/8 inch hole ¾ inch into the heel, measuring 5/8 inch from the outer edge of the rafter. Drill a second hole at the top 60 degree cut, measuring 1 1/8" from the bottom of the angle. These two holes will be used to receive the dowels in the top plate and the rafter ring.

Lay the rafter flat, and measure a point 1.5 inch perpendicular and 1.5 inches parallel from the inside point of the 30 degree cut heel. Drill a ¼ inch hole through the rafter. The aircraft cable will be strung through the holes that you drill in each rafter, once the rafters are installed.

Time: 4.5 hours
Material List:
2" by 4", 8' lengths – 25
2" by 2", 8' lengths (for snow load regions) – 8
Screws, 3" – 1.5 lb
Dowels, 3/8" - 50

H. The Rafter Ring

The roof ring on this specific yurt is easily constructed and relatively lightweight. Cut two 24" circles from either 7/16 inch OSB or 3/8 plywood. The easiest way to ensure accuracy of your cut is to draw two diagonal lines, each running from one corner to the opposite corner of a twenty-four inch by twenty-four inch square of material. Drill a screw into the centre where the two lines intersect, and, using a piece of string attached at the screw, hold a carpenter's pencil at the 24" mark on the string. Now, scribe a circle holding the pencil at the mark as you rotate around the piece of wood. Remove the screw.

Now cut twenty-five pieces of 2 by 4 to 4 inches long. Set your mitre saw to 15 (14.5 actual) degrees, and (being careful to keep your fingers clear of the blade!), cut each piece into a 3.12 inch width by 4" length. Lay out the pieces flat around the circumference of one circle that you have already cut, with the wide end pointed toward the centre of the circle. The flat wide edge of each piece should rest against the outer lip of the board, so that the centre point of the 3.12 inch width is precisely against the outside of the circle. Work your way around the circumference, placing each subsequent piece in order. You may have to trim the final piece to fit.

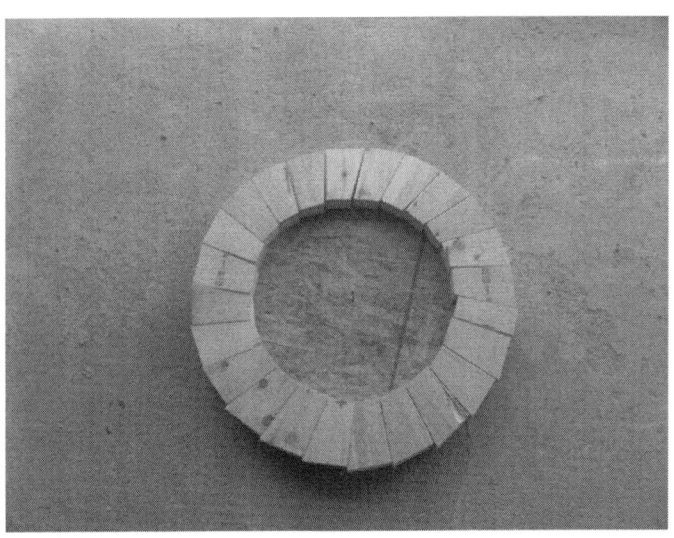

Next, lay the second circle precisely in line with the first, on top of the 25 pieces. Carefully screw one 1 ½ screw three inches from the outer edge of each piece through the OSB into each tapered block. Making sure that you hold the bottom circle tightly in place against the upper pieces, flip the structure over and screw one screw into each block through this OSB circle, as you did on the flip side. Locate the centre of the circle again. Measure a square six inches on each side, using the centre point as the centre of this square. Drill 3/8 inch holes at each corner, then, using your jig saw, cut out the square of material. Repeat the process or the other side by drilling down from the corners of the cut-out through the other circle, and then cutting the square of material out. This will ensure that the two squares line up.

Cut four pieces of 2 by 2, with each piece fitting into the spaces around the cut-out between the two circles, so that the box is closed in. Screw the pieces in place.

Measure 1 ½ inch from one edge of each 3 1/8 inch block. Measure 1 1/8 inch up from the bottom of the bottom circle of OSB to a point that intersects the 1 ½ inch mark. Drill a 3/8" hole ¾ inch deep at this point for each block, glue and insert a dowel in each hole. Allow to dry.

Cut a piece of 1.5 inch thick rigid insulation into a 24 inch square. Using foam insulation adhesive, glue this piece in place on top of the rafter ring so that the entire circle is covered. Let adhesive dry. Next, angling your saw or thick-edge knife at a 30 degree slope (approximate) inward toward the centre of the circle, cut the edge of the insulation around the circle so that the insulation now is circular and sloped to the same angle as the yurt roof (30 degrees). Cut a second circle of insulation, with the diameter the same as the top of the glued piece. Glue it to the layer already affixed to the rafter ring. Once the adhesive has dried, cut it on an angle in the same manner as the first piece. Now, cut out the square piece, using the rafter ring square vent hole as a guide.

The purpose of this double layer of insulation is twofold: to keep the intense heat of the sun on the roof to a minimum and to provide a base on wish to install the dome vent so that the maximum vent space is provided while preventing wind and rain from swirling under the dome vent and into the yurt.

Time: 1.5 hours
Material List:
2" by 4", 8' lengths – 1
OSB, 7/16 inch, 4' by 8' sheet – ¼ sheet
Screws, 2" - .25 lb
1.5" insulation, 4' by 8' sheet – ¼ sheet

Installing the yurt rafter ring.

If your walls are not level and vertical, and if your platform similarly is not level, you will encounter difficulty when installing the rafters and rafter ring. One of the most common problems is that the rafters do not meet precisely at the rafter ring, or that the ring tends to slant to one side or the other. Additionally, if the king post does not hold the ring in precise position, and if you do not line up the rafters correctly to the ring, it will tend to spiral out of position (see sample photo below). For these reasons, it is imperative that you pay attention to detail when installing the rafters and ring.

With the ring in position, line up the first rafter so that it meets the ring at a 90 degree angle to the face of the ring. Make sure that the dowel is fully inserted in the rafter at the ring and at the heel of the rafter on the top plate. Use a scrap piece of 1 by four or 1 by 6, about a foot in length. Screw two screws spaced about six inches apart through the scrap material into the rafter, and then two screws through the scrap into the bottom of the rafter ring, making sure that the rafter remains at right angles to the face of the ring edge.

Move to a position opposite the first rafter on the rafter ring. Count to make sure that the number of spaces between the top of the rafter at the rafter ring is the same as the spaces between the two rafters at the top plates. Put this rafter in place in the same manner as the first (again, make sure that the ring has not moved out of position). Now, repeat the process for a rafter approximately 90 degrees around the ring from the second rafter and midway between the second and first. Similarly, install the fourth rafter at a point one quarter of the way around the ring circle. All should fit properly, if the wall segments are vertical and the floor platform is level. Install the remaining rafters, working your way around by installing each rafter about one quarter of the way around the ring from the prior rafter. You most likely will be unable to install temporary bracing for all of the rafters.

Keep the temporary supports in place until the roof insulation, tarpaulin and roof vent are installed, to maintain structural integrity. Once the tarp, insulation and vent are in place, remove the temporary bracing, one at a time, replacing each one with a four inch by ¾ inch wide metal strap or mending plate, secured by two screws to the bottom of the rafter and two to the rafter ring.

Cut a circular piece of rigid insulation the diameter of the bottom of the rafter ring, and screw it into place on the bottom of the rafter ring, using 2.5 inch screws with washers (to prevent the screws from pulling through the insulation). Cut out and opening in the insulation that coincides with the opening in the rafter ring.

One of the many reasons why I chose to focus on this basic yurt design is the ease with which the rafter ring can be raised into place by one person. Usually, raising and holding the rafter ring in place while rafters are secured requires a minimum of two people or costly and time-consuming temporary equipment. As the diameter of a yurt increases, so does its apex. Similarly, as the pitch of the roof increases, height of the peak does as well. That means that a typical sixteen foot yurt with seven foot walls and a 45 degree rise would require a temporary king post structure, to hold the rafter ring in place, that would need to be fourteen feet tall. A twenty-four foot yurt with a thirty degree rise would need a fifteen foot king post, and a twenty-eight foot yurt with the same slope would need a sixteen foot king post. While each of these one-time use apparatus would require several hours to build, the king post for the sixteen foot, 30 degree slope, seven-foot wall yurt needs nothing more than a 12 foot length of 1 ½ inch ABS plumbing pipe and four $3 pulleys! This king post allows you to raise the rafter ring by inserting the pulleys on the top end of the pipe and stringing rope through them to points on the rafter ring (resting in the centre of the yurt floor), and pulling on the ropes to raise the rafter ring to its proper height and position.

To begin the process, obtain three 8-foot lengths of 2 by four, and screw a 2 ½ inch screw halfway into a point about six inches from the top of each 2 by 4. Insert a long screw about half its length into a point that is precisely in the centre of the floor, at the point where the centre of the rafter ring would rest.

Put the rafter ring on the floor so that the screw is located at the centre of the vent opening. Stand the abs pipe so that the end of it is over top of this screw and the pipe is standing inside the vent opening of the rafter ring. Stand the three two-by-fours, with their "foot" ends inside the vent opening, around the vertical abs pipe, and, using a length of rope, tie these four items together, with the rope snug under the protruding screws. Slowly spread the 2 by 4 "legs" apart from the pole and equidistant from each other, lifting the rafter ring by hand or using the ropes and pulley assemblies so that the legs of the 2 by 4s can spread. With the legs spread at least three feet from the centre pole, use a screw that is sufficient length to fasten the floor end of each leg to the floor.

The rafter ring should be resting on the apex of the three legs and the pole. Using the rope and pulleys, raise the rafter ring to its proper height and tie off the ropes to hold the ring in place.

With the channel to the top of the rafter, and the 30 degree slope to the bottom, align the first rafter so that the dowel at the top plate and the dowel at the rafter ring fit snugly into the holes cut into the rafter. Toenail two screws through the top end of the rafter into the rafter ring, and one through the heel end of the rafter into the top plate.

Cut eight 12 inch lengths of 2 by 4. Using your mitre saw, cut an angle that is 150 degrees (30 degrees of one side) in each piece. Using 2 ½ inch screws secure one piece to the underside of a rafter so that the cut edge fits snugly against the rafter and the bottom of the OSB on the rafter ring. Install the remaining seven pieces in similar manner, spaced equidistant around the perimeter of the rafter ring. (This provides additional downward support for the rafter ring). As an alternative, you may use steel strapping or ties to connect the rafter to the ring from underneath.

Once each of the rafters has been put in place and securely fastened, the king pole assembly can be removed and reused for your plumbing or drainage needs.

To cut the insulation, it is recommended that you first assemble the rafters according to the assembly instruction at the end of this guide, so that you can ensure that each piece fits precisely.

If you have cut the rafters, top plates and wall segments correctly, the insulation will be 23 inches wide at the base, tapering to 2.75 inch wide at the peak, and 93 inches long. It should look like an elongated isosceles triangle. To minimize waste material, use a 4 by 8 foot sheet of insulation, and mark the first piece with the 23 width from the outer edge, and the second measured from the opposite outer edge. This will allow you to cut a third piece from the centre material. A fourth segment can be salvaged by using the two right triangle remnants together, if needed.

Installing roof insulation

The size and shape of the roof insulation panels is designed to maximize the amount of material used in each 4' by 8' sheet of foam insulation, with minimal waste. However, the panels also form a relatively tight-fitting moisture-repelling vapour barrier. These pieces, triangular in shape, also insert easily into the slots cut in each rafter, and can be replaced quite easily, even when the roof tarpaulin is in place.

However, installing the panels prior to putting the roof tarpaulin over top is the recommended process. Simply lay them in place from the outside or inside, and, using a length of board, press any panels that are a slightly tighter fit into place in the channels cut in the roof rafters.

Should you wish to install additional reflective moisture barrier inside, you may staple mylar-backed bubble insulation (it comes in rolls 3 or 4 feet wide, and lengths up to 50 feet) to the bottom side of the rafters. Seal the joints using foil tape, available at most lumber stores.

If you are installing concealed electrical wires (e.g. for lights, fans and outlets), you should run these wires along the inside edges of the rafters where needed prior to installing the foil-backed interior insulation.

Time: 2 hours
Materials:
1.5" thick rigid insulation, 4' by 8' sheet – 8 sheets

I. The Dome Vent

The vent is exceptionally easy to construct. Cut four triangular pieces of 7/16 OSB, with the bases 23 inches and height of each of the equal sides of the isosceles triangles 219 inches each. This will use up a 24" by 48" piece of material. Cut four pieces of 2" by 2" 19 inches long, with a 60 degree angle at one end. Cut two pieces of 2" by 2" twenty-four inches long, with 30 degree cuts sloping inward at each end. Cut one piece of those two at the 11 ¼ inch point and cut the remaining piece so it is the same length. Cut a piece of 1" by 6" scrap material to approximately six inches in length. Cut a piece of tarpaulin approximately 36 inches by 36 inches. Cut a piece of fibreglass screen into a square that is twenty-five inches on each side.

Join the three pieces with the 30 degree cuts as shown in the photo below, to form a cross shape and screw the 1" by 6" piece into each of the arms where they meet.

Cut away the excess material from the 1" by 6" piece as shown below.

Join the four pieces with the 60 degree cuts as shown in the photo below to form a pyramid, with the 60 degree cuts meeting at the apex.
Screws the cross-shape beneath the legs as shown. So that the 30 degree cuts fit snugly against each leg.

Screw each of the triangles of OSB onto the structure as shown below, closing in the pyramid from the top.

Staple the screen in place underneath the dome vent, in line and flat against the cross structure, with all edges stapled against the inside of the OSB.

Lay out a section of tarpaulin that is 36 inches by 36 inches. With the centre of the tarp resting on the peak of the dome, fold one edge over the bottom lip of one side of the dome, and staple the tarp inside the vent side. Repeat for the adjacent sides. This will leave a surplus of material on the fourth side. Fold the excess under itself in the same manner as you would for a gift-wrapped box. Holding the material in place, insert a bead of silicone caulk in the fold, press into place, and staple the fold flat. Run a bead of clear caulk over the staples, so that they are waterproofed. Staple the edge of this fourth side under the edge of the OSB.

Time: 1.5 hr.
Material List:
2" by 2", 8' lengths – 1
OSB, 7/16", 4' by 8' sheet – ¼ sheet
Screws, 2" – ¼ lb
Fiberglass screen – 9 sq ft

Raising the yurt dome vent

The roof vent will be raised into place from the outside of the building. Wrap the assembly in fabric so that, as it is raised, it does not snag on or puncture the roof tarpaulin. Tie the bundle with a rope and drop the rope through the roof rafter opening. (This may be more easily accomplished by tying a smooth weight that is not too heavy to the rope and tossing it out the vent hole from the inside, instead of trying to accurately throw the rope into the hole from the exterior. Attach the rope that is thrown from the inside to the wrapped vent assembly.
Pull the vent into a position on top of the rafter ring and stand it in position so that it sits uniformly over the opening. Using four lengths of one by two, attaché the vent to the roof rafter by screwing the 1*2s to each inside corner of the rafter opening and securing those 1 by 2s to the cross members of the vent assembly.

Installing the tarpaulin skins

Prior to installation of the skins, inspect the wall segments for gaps and distortion. Although the wall panels structurally are capable of carrying significant loads, they are very light, and subject to warp. For this reason, we recommend that you either install dowels between adjacent panels at the 48 inch point from the bottom plate, or use package strapping, stapled into place around the perimeter of the yurt at the same point on the wall segments. This will draw the individual units together. To install, apply tape overlapping the panel adjacent to where you wish to begin the tape. Staple the tape on the stud of that adjacent panel, and draw the panels together before continuing the application of the tape around the perimeter of the yurt. Repeat the process of drawing the panels together, applying the tape and stapling into the studs until the taping is complete.

You may fill any gaps between the panels with mastic, rope caulk or fibreglass insulation. If you are installing the yurt permanently on site, you may opt to use spray foam insulation, and trim the cured foam to fit. There will be a few joints in the plates and the panels that do not fit precisely. To eliminate air flow, and to deter pests, fill these gaps similarly.

To install the exterior skin, begin at one side of the door frame. Screw the first 7' edge of the wall tarp aligned tightly against the edge of the door frame. Making sure that the upper edge of the tarp is stretched tight and is straight, secure the top edge of the tarpaulin around the upper perimeter of the wall, securing it to the top plate with 1" drywall screws and washers spaces eighteen inches apart. If the walls are constructed properly and erected plum (vertical), the tarp should fall evenly along the wall. Continue around the perimeter until you reach the other side of the door jamb, where you will secure the end of the tarpaulin.

Now, move around the exterior of the building again, smoothing out any irregularities or creases in the tarpaulin and fastening the tarp at the bottom plate of the wall. While this usually is adequate to secure the wall skin, you may opt to use ratchet straps joined together to wrap around the entire bottom of the wall, holding this tarp securely and providing additional barrier to rodent infiltration.

Locate the first window opening. Cut 1 ½ inches in from the window frame to remove the excess material in the opening. Now, slice at 45 degrees from each corner toward the centre. Fold back the fabric on the lower horizontal part of the frame against the window frame and staple it in place. Do the same for each side. Now run a bead of caulking along the outside lip of the window opening on top of the tarp on the bottom and sides of the frame. Slide the window into place, making sure that the tarp on the upper edge of the window overlaps the window. Lift this flap of material back, and apply a bead of caulk between the window and the tarp, screw the window into place and press the tarp flap into the bead of caulk. Repeat this process for the next two windows.

To install the umbrella roof skin, first tie ropes in several of the eyelets of the tarp, with each length of rope being at least 30 feet long. Secure a small weight to the other end of the ropes. Roll the tarp so that you have formed a long, cigar-like bundle. Pass the weighted end of the ropes through the roof rafter ring vent, so that a person on the outside can grab the ends of the rope. Now, pulling the ropes so that the open end of the roof tarp emerges first through the vent opening. As the tarp is pulled through the opening (being very careful not to snag or puncture the tarp), separate the lengths of rope from each other and pull the tarp simultaneously from opposite sides of the yurt. The tarp should mushroom out like an umbrella.

The alternative to this method is to drag the tarp over the roof structure from the outside. However, this is a cumbersome and difficult process, often leading to tears in the fabric.

Once the tarpaulin is fitted over the roof rafters, attach a rope to the insulation dome (if it is not aready affixed to the rafter ring), and pull it up, from the outside, between the tarp and the rafter assembly. You will have to work this cone into place carefully from inside the yurt, by reaching through the vent opening and manoeuvring it into place.

Now, screw eyes into the platform around the exterior perimeter of the yurt, approximately two inches form the yurt walls and spaced the same distance apart as the eyelets in the roof tarp. Using ¼ inch nylon rope, run the ropes from each eyelet, through each eye below it, up to the next eyelet, down through the next eye, and so on, until the ropes pass through every eyelet and every eye. Work your way around the perimeter, drawing this rope snug. It is this rope that holds the roof tarp in place. As with the wall trap, you may wish to install ratchet straps around the upper perimeter of the wall, holding the roof tarp tightly in place against the top plate.
Time: .75 hr
Materials:
roof tarpaulin (custom), wall tarpaulin (custom) – 1
1.5 inch screw-in eyes – 24
3/8" nylon rope – 150 feet.

Installing the aircraft cable.

Installation of the 1/8 inch by 50 foot aircraft cable is essential to draw all rafters into a circle, and to offset the outward pressure of the rafter heels on the walls. Drill ¼ inch holes in each rafter, 1.5 inches from the bottom of the heel and 1.0 inches in from the wall. Thread the cable through these holes. Fasten a turnbuckle to one end of the cable, using a u-bolt clamp. Open the turnbuckle and clamp the other end of the cable to the turnbuckle. Tighten the turnbuckle until the cable is taut, but not so tight as to place too much strain on the rafters.

To hang the interior curtain wall tarpaulin, use s-hooks, hung from the cable and through each eyelet of the tarpaulin. This curtain wall can be cut into segments so that the curtain can slide back or forward to act as drapery over the individual windows.
Time: ½ hr.
Materials:
3/16" aircraft cable – 50'
6" turnbuckle – 1
3/16" cable clamps - 2

Interior Finish

You will notice that there is a gap between the top plate and the bottom of the roof insulation. There are two techniques that I recommend to fill these spaces, one of which is very simple and quick, but that does not maximize insulative value of the filler and the other which requires more time and diligence.

The first requires that you cut four inch widths of rigid insulation that are the same lengths as the space between each rafter at the top plate (optimally, twenty-tow and one half inch). Screw each of these pieces between the rafters against the top plate, using one screw and washer for each piece (make sure that the foil side is exposed to the inside of the yurt).

The second requires that you cut pieces the same length as in the first method, but that also are cut at a 30 degree angle sloping front to back on the piece, and then cut to a width that will allow the piece to slide snugly into the space between the bottom of the roof insulation and the top plate, between the rafters.

The yurt, as it currently is designed, will not meet the National Fire Code Standards for flame retardant capacity for residential buildings. However, you may opt to use polystyrene or polyurethane rigid insulation that incorporates fire retardants, and may choose to apply a tarpaulin treated with fire retardant over the interior walls. Another option is to use a commercially available fire retardant spray. Many outdoor equipment suppliers carry a spray that is a combination of waterproofing and fire retardant. This may seem to be relevant only to exterior applications, but interior waterproofing acts as a light duty vapour barrier. One other option to reduced flame spread is to apply aluminum foil liner, or foil backed insulation to the inside of the yurt walls, particularly on the ceiling or roof. There is an added benefit to foil application: the reflective surface cuts down on the amount of ambient lighting required in the structure!

Time: 1-1.5 hr
Materials: scrap insulation pieces

Building washrooms

Washrooms pose a problem in yurts. Not so much because of the plumbing, but because they substantially decrease the energy efficiency of the building.

The primary reason that yurts are so economical to heat and so cozy is because there are not "dead" spots of trapped air in corners, simply because there are no corners! Air moves freely, meaning that temperatures are remarkably the same everywhere in the yurt, even with the wind blowing outside, if the structure is built properly. By installing walls, you stop or restrict air movement, and cold spots result. In addition, those cold spots also encourage condensation. The best washroom wall, therefore, is no wall at all. This can be a significant problem for the majority of us who are too modest and too reluctant to use the facilities in the open.

An easy option is the moveable (and removable) curtain wall. Simply use drapery on suspected tracks or aircraft cable strung across the height of the building to partition off the washroom area when in use. Hang tarpaulin or drapery fabric (it is heavier than tarp) using s-hooks through the tarp eyelets and over the aircraft cable, and pull back these curtains when not in use. No need for doors, no air flow impediment. Need a shower? Again, use a retractable curtain that encircles the tub or shower space, and pull back those curtains when not in use.

Time: varied
Materials:

Total Time:
Approximately 28-32 hours construction, 3-4 hours assembly, 2 hours disassembly

Total Material List:
1" by 6", 8' – 36
1" by 3", 8' – 48
(or substitute 26 2" by 6", 8' for above two items)
Screws, 2" – 3 lb
1.5 inch thick 4' by 8' rigid insulation – 28 ¼
Carpenter's glue – 1 pint
7/16" OSB, 4' by 8' – 8.5

2" by 2", 8' – 29
1" by 2", 8' – 46
Screws, 3 ½" – 2.5 lb
3/8" staples – 1,000 (1 pk)
Mini-glue sticks – 27
Package strapping – 50'
3/8" dowels – 119
Medium duty tarp – 72-77 sq. yd
2" by 8", 8' – 4
2" by 4", 8' – 39
Shed windows – 3
Prehung steel door – 1
Screws, 3" – 1.75 lb
Fiberglass screen – 1 sq yd
Dome tarp, custom – 1
Exterior wall tarp, custom – 1
Interior wall tarp, custom – 1
3/8" nylon rope – 150 ft
Medium screw eyes – 24
Aircraft cable, 3/16" – 50 ft
Turnbuckle, 6" – 1
3/16" cable clamps – 2
Right angle steel supports (3" by 3") - 6

Plumbing & Responsible Water Use

While my wife and I have adopted a minimalist strategy toward the use of the earth's resources, we, too, are not excused from using this precious water frugally. In our first yurt, we have, however, minimized our consumption to less than 150-225 litres of water per week (7,800 litres per year). That's almost 2,000 cubic feet of water, or 1,000 cubic feet per person, compared to the North American average of over 5 times that amount per individual (not including industry), we should be proud of our ecological stewardship. However, we found that, while we have had difficulty in using less, we have been able to recycle and reuse more. In the summer, our grey water, from our shower, kitchen sink and bathroom sink is routed into a 230-litre holding tank, and then used, each week, to water our gardens. In the early spring and late fall, we use some of that water in a sprayer system to "flush" our toilet, using less than two cups per flush.

A channel dug around the perimeter of our yurt redirects rainfall into a small dugout pond, where it, too, can be used for the gardens. With water consumption for our vegetable cooking, we, again, have discovered ways to minimize, by using minimal water for boiling potatoes, then using that water to steam or cook our vegetables. That enriched water, in turn, is used to make soups and stews, and excess potato water is used to make bread. For the few times that we boil eggs, the water is mixed with other water (sometimes rainwater), for washing dishes.

One of the concerns that people have expressed is that we may be transferring bacteria and water-borne disease by reusing some of our water in dish cleaning, and, again, on the gardens. However, the eggs are hard shelled, and harbour no bacteria that is resistant to the dish soap. On the other hand, because our grey water sits in the holding tank for up to seven days, there is a risk of bacteria build-up. Consequently, we make sure that we water our plants only at the base or roots, so that there is a minimal risk of contamination.

Other factors also come into play. The odour from stale water is not pleasant, but, within an hour after watering any residual odour has dissipated. If you add glycol (RV antifreeze) to the tanks in the winter, this water should not be used on the plants, as glycol is extremely hazardous to human health. On the other hand, if you have used less than 5% antifreeze per tank, that liquid can safely be applied to the roots of larger trees.

One final tip: when installing our grey water holding tank, we constructed it so that the tank was below the level of the shower and sink drains, but above grade, so that we could siphon, easily, the water from the tank, relying on the benefit of gravity to move the water.

Perhaps, in the near future, we will be able to purify the water, recycle it for human use (washing, etc.) and then apply it to the garden. That will cut our consumption in half. However, using only the minimal amount required does offer a measure of environmental responsibility that should make any of us employing these measures confident that we are doing our part to protect the environment.

Black water and waste are more complex issues.

Rather than spend upwards of $8,000 to $10,000 for a well that would have limited use (we consume less than 30 litres (7.5 gallons) of water daily) and would require lots of energy for the pressure pump, we haul our water weekly from a nearby artesian well and store it in a 100-gallon PVC tank. It is pumped by a 12 volt RV water pump, through pex line, to a propane-powered tankless water heater. Our total cost for hot water over a four month period was twenty pounds of propane!

Waste is broken into two components: grey water and black water (sewage). As indicated, we used a 45-gallon (235 litre) tank to collect our grey water. The toilet feeds into another 45-gallon tank that sits directly below the toilet. That tank is pumped regularly, using a mascerator, into other tanks, and removed to a remote location where the waste is composted using solar heat blankets and a 12 volt fan to vent it. After a year, the compost is used to feed the naturally occurring bush and trees on the property.

Initially, our composting toilet system wasn't letting the waste fall readily into the accumulator. That problem, we discovered, was caused because we used too little water to wash the solids through. A minimum of two cups of water is required to flush the waste out of the toilet bowl properly. We now keep a small plant sprayer filled with water next to the toilet, to rinse out excess materials when needed.

The plumbing used for both the black water and grey water systems is minimal.

Our kitchen sink is connected directly from the cold water line and from the outlet of the tankless water heater, using pex lines. Branching off from these two lines, two lines connect to the bathroom sink. Branching off from the bathroom sink, the cold water line feeds into the RV toilet (which has been modified to use less water and is part of the composting system previously described). The hot water line branches off to the shower.

Note that there is only a hot water line to the shower. The shower "tap" consists of nothing more than an inline shutoff valve. There is no temperature control at the shower. Instead, we use the various settings (large flame/small flame, large flow/small flow, summer/winter) settings on the tankless water heater to govern the temperature of the water at the shower head. It is surprisingly effective, and takes less time than it does to find the precise temperature at the shower head with conventional taps. It also costs about ¼ of the price and uses less pipe.

Ingenuity is required, if you intend to live off the grid, live in an eco-friendly manner, and live cost-effectively. But the efforts are well worth the results achieved.

Lighting

In our first yurt, by laying a reflective white light-duty panelling over the interior walls, we reduced the need for lighting. Four 18" x 48" mirrors were placed around the perimeter to reflect light, as well. We "traded in our three halogen floor lamps (250 watts each) for three LED 1.5 watt energy efficient lights!. Now, our entire lighting consists of a 5-arm floor lamp with 1.5-watt LEDs, 20 solar lights marking our exterior entrance and walkway, one LED puck light over the entrance inside the yurt, and four plug-in LED light packs, producing as much light, each, as a 60 watt incandescent bulb, but drawing a total of 13 watts of energy for all of them.
Since living in a yurt implies living in an area where zoning and building code restrictions do not impede construction, many yurts must be designed to operate "off the grid." Off the grid, for our yurt, is exactly that: no electrical supply grid, no wired Internet access, no wired telephone and no community water services infrastructure. All of these services, however, have been incorporated into our yurt infrastructure design, as standalone systems.
Electrical services, for most of us, offer the greatest challenge, both in terms of economics and supply. We use three sources of power: wind, water pressure, solar and backup generator.
Solar is the easiest to install, with an array of commercial solar panels that provide modest amounts of power. Unfortunately, in our northern latitudes, winter solar potential exists for less than eight hours per day, while, in summer, we receive fifteen hours of sunlight energy.
Wind power also is available readily, with 1.5kw wind turbines costing less than $1,000. We opted to design our own, using automotive alternators and a homebuilt vertical turbine structure. Even with these systems, peak demand often exceeds supply, and we have installed a battery array of eight 12-volt deep cycle batteries and a 1,000 watt inverter.
It is the inverter system that offers a variety of options, from cheap to pricey, from ineffective to potentially damaging to safe and sufficient.

Most of the budget inverters on the market are modified sine wave inverters. For most applications, these inverters work well. However, with sophisticated electronics, including computers or LED and plasma televisions, a pure sine wave system is the only safe and viable option. Unfortunately, they are three to four times the cost of a modified sine wave inverter.

One attractive option is to use both modified and pure sine wave inverters in your design.

We use a 12-volt pump to pressure our internal water supply. It is connected directly to our battery pack, as is our low-demand led lighting for the bathroom and entrance. We move dead air that pools in some areas of the yurt, using 12-volt computer fans, also connected directly to the battery array. In almost all of our other day-to-day electrical needs, we use less than 300 watts, for lighting, radio, charging small devices and to charge the laptop computer. For these applications, we use a 300-watt inverter, costing under $75.

But, we also power a 43-watt cooler (sometimes two of them), 24 hours per day, and our television (which sees less than ½ hour of use each day, even in the winter). When our laptop is operating on electrical power, it consumes 90 watts. Two of these items require pure sine wave inversion, so we use a 1,000 watt pure sine wave inverter. This system costs around $300.

Ironically, using less electricity by relying on 12-volt collection methods and inverters actually costs a nominal amount of power. Like a DVD player on standby, an inverter consumes very small amounts of energy, even when no appliances or power draws are connected to it. Consequently, whether you are using pure or modified wave systems, you should turn off those units when not needed, to conserve battery power.

While it is quite easy to live "off the grid" in your yurt, it is a lifestyle that requires adaptation and planning, as well as an understanding of the demands of your home, each hour of the day. Integral to that planning is knowing what type of system you need, for what type of equipment you will be powering. Simply hooking up a few small solar panels to one or two 12-volt batteries and a couple of cigar lighter inverters is highly unlikely to offer you any chance of success!

Being eco-friendly may be admirable, but it comes with a price, and it is not always as crystal-clear as one believes.

We rely heavily on non-grid energy, including wind and solar power. However, renewal energy sources such as ours require energy storage, and, specifically, battery storage. While there are advanced battery technologies on the market (e.g. batteries for hybrid vehicles), as well as large wet-cell storage batteries (such as those in forklifts and indoor industrial cleaning equipment), the most prevalent, and therefore, the lowest-priced units are conventional deep-cycle marine 12-volt batteries. These typically cost from $80 to $200, with only modest storage and cranking amperage.

The primary advantage of marine batteries over vehicle batteries is their capacity to be discharged to low levels and recharged often. However, "often" is subjective, with most of the commercially available units being rated for a few hundred charging cycles, at most. These batteries also do not like to be frozen, but really detest excessive heat.

In order to supply minimal energy, such as the energy to light two compact fluorescent bulbs four hours each day and a small bar refrigerator (drawing 90 watts, with a surge of 800 watts), you will consume 2,280 (2.3 kw) watts each day. Now consider that a small solar panel produces 13-18 watts (some of the single panel retail units produce 30w) under optimal conditions. In northern latitudes, hours of summer daylight average 15 hours, but typically generate only about 60% of that in sunlight sufficient to "max out" the solar panel. With three panels, you will produce 405 watts – less than 20% of what you need. A small wind turbine may produce 40% of what you need, if you live in an environment where the wind is very frequent, and of sufficient strength to power the turbine. Typically, the marine batteries attached to your collectors are rated for 800-1000 CCA. Obviously, unless you expand your generation and/or storage network, you will need to use a charging system on the batteries.

Because each of the batteries is being discharged the equivalent of 100% every eight hours, you will require a battery array of at least three batteries, just to produce your daily minimum energy requirement. Ultimately, most of us will require electricity for television or sound equipment, charging cell phones and laptops, power for small fans, and so on. With minimal energy, though, your three-battery array will be fully discharged and recharged 100 times from June to September. That is the normal lifespan of the battery! This year, we experienced near-record heat and sunlight throughout our summer. While that is great for our solar panels, heat is more damaging to the batteries than cold, and reduces their ability to be recharged (and hold a charge) significantly.

We used an eight-battery package. However, almost weekly, we needed to refill the cells, as the electrolytic acid evaporated. The sunlight did its damage, too, destroying one battery. Of the eight, only one battery now holds a significant charge, even though I de-sulphated the batteries regularly. Five of the batteries were three years old or less, with the other three being four years old. Seven batteries will need to be replaced.

At a cost of $90 per battery, our outlay will be $630, plus taxes. We used nearly $100 of generator fuel to supplement our renewable energy supply. In four months, our lighting costs will be $700-800, factoring in the wear and tear on equipment.

Now, we have batteries that need to be recycled and spent fuel that polluted the air. If we had relied on our hydro-electric grid for energy, at a cost of $0.08 per kwh, we would have spent less than $130! Did we really do the environment and our pocketbook a favour?

Most often, power is not an issue. Good quality wind turbines that will generate 1-3 kilowatts cost less than $1,000. Solar panels can be purchased with price tags that are lower than $4 per watt output. Battery storage options are varied, with an array of deep cycle marine batteries the most common option. Good, used electric forklift batteries offer tons of storage at low cost. Power inverters (use two) cost $150-300, with modified sine wave being the cheapest and pure sine wave, necessary for sophisticated and delicate electronic equipment such as televisions and computers, being the more expensive choice.

Heating

Heat, too, is relatively simple. In our original yurt, we used a combination of heat sources, including radiant propane, kerosene (biodiesel) heaters and outdoor wood furnace.

The outdoor wood furnace is a simple design, using a steel 45-gallon barrel filled with water over an enclosed wood-fired heat source. The enclosure is cinder block filled with sand. Steel piping leads from the barrel, underground to the yurt, where it is fed through three small truck radiators spaced around the room. Heat is circulated using 12 volt fans on the radiators. While it was not required, we use a small RV water pump to circulate the water. The design is such that the force of expanding hot water in the pipes moves the water sufficiently up the slope to the yurt, while the cooled water returns to the system via gravity. A one-way valve ensures that it flows properly.

Using just the propane radiant heaters, with spring & fall average temperatures at night averaging -5 C, and daytime highs at 10C, twenty pounds of propane lasts 10-12 days.

Heat for cooking comes from a recycled RV propane stove. We cook two to three months on less than 20 pounds of propane.

These radiant heaters were sufficient for keeping the yurt warm during nights when the temperature dipped to minus 25. Indeed, we used only one radiant heater, and needed to shut it off around 2 or 3 a.m., because the yurt was too warm!

As a backup, we had a 30,000 BTU kerosene heater available. Instead of using kerosene, we opted for a more environmentally friendly biodiesel (which we made ourselves). The output gases provide much better air quality, as well.

Our mirror reflectors (discussed in the Tips & Issues section, provided improved lighting and modest amounts of reflected solar heat.

By moving our furniture around and using dark drapery on the windows, we trapped additional solar heat with the darker materials acting as heat sinks.

Yurt Flooring

In keeping with the minimal philosophy of living in a yurt, the ideal design will employ a minimum of materials, be as "green" as possible and will be both sustainable and durable.

In the yurt design that we have described earlier, we used OSB as the only subfloor. Conventional homes use a subfloor and underlay layer, installed crosswise to each other. This brings considerable weight to the structure. To reduce weight demand, we used the single layer, relying on the rigid insulation installed directly underneath to provide added strength. This leaves us with more options for finished flooring.

The recommended finish for the yurt you have constructed is to lay down a membrane of vinyl (pool liner or tarpaulin) covering the OSB, followed by a top application of indoor/outdoor carpeting. On the portions of the platform that are exposed to the exterior elements, this is important, as OSB deteriorates rapidly in moist conditions, and requires protection from the rain and snow. Simply ensure that the bottom of the wall tarp skins overlap on top of the membrane and carpet, so that moisture does not pool around the perimeter., As an added precaution, drill ½ inch holes about every three feet around the wall perimeter (about 1 inch from the wall) through the OSB and rigid insulation in the platform, to allow water to drain quickly.

In our first yurt, we chose a very inexpensive, basic design and material for our flooring. There are several reasons for this.

Firstly, cost is a factor in the decision as to the type of flooring to use. We opted for materials with a cost of less than $0.45 per square foot, plus $0.10 per square foot for finishes.

Secondly, we wanted to ensure that the frequent traffic directly from outdoors to indoors did not track in excess dirt. Carpeting would have trapped that dirt.

Thirdly, the location of the yurt in a wooded area would have attracted insects such as ants. By constructing flooring with a hard surface, we eliminated nesting sites for those insects.

Fourthly, we wanted a floor that would remain cool in the summer and able to adapt to winter conditions. With the hard surface, we were able to lay down area carpets that we already owned in strategic locations, while keeping bare floor at entrances and frequently used work areas, such as the kitchen areas and washroom.

Lastly, we wanted to minimize weight of the flooring, since we built the yurt on pads and posts, rather than embedding pillars into the ground.

To accomplish all four goals, we used ¾ inch oriented strand board as sub floor material, with 1/8 inch good one side plywood laid at a ninety degree angles to the subfloor as the main floor. The plywood was screwed to the underlay using three quarter inch wood screws with threads the full length of the screw. The use of full-length threads is essential, so that the screws can be countersunk into the thin plywood.

Lastly, we used a clear varnish to coat the surface of the flooring, making sure to pay special attention to the high traffic areas.

Since installing this flooring, we have found that it works remarkably well, and shows a sheen and grain similar to good-quality hardwood or laminate flooring, at one quarter of the cost. However, some problems have arisen. On occasion, we stored 20 pound propane tanks on the floor, and, with changing temperatures, the tanks attracted condensation. This condensation accumulated in a ring on the floor. To remove it, we lightly scoured the area with a Javex and water mix, with modest success. The only other problem has been a slight separation, due to the thinness of the material, in spots where insufficient screws were used.

This flooring has answered all five of our criteria for the design, and is recommended for anyone contemplating an inexpensive flooring alternative, whether in a yurt or cabin.

Perimeter drainage

Spring had proven to be a real test for our yurt. To close out the late fall and early winter, we experienced exceptionally unusual rainfall and early snowfall. Because we have built our yurt on the slope of a hill, the deck on which the yurt rests is at ground level at the rear, and fifty-four inches off the ground in the front. This permits good air flow, but demanded that we hoard the perimeter to block cold air infiltration. Unfortunately, the hoarding also trapped humidity, and we experienced numerous condensation issues throughout November and the first week of December.
The interior of the yurt is lined with foil-backed bubble insulation, with all joints taped. This makes for a very air-tight unit, but any moisture inside is trapped, as well. Cooking, showering and even everyday living contributes to the high humidity. We experimented with a number of options to reduce this wet air, with limited success.
The major problem was that, because it was winter, we needed to seal and insulate our rooftop vent. This creates a dome where the heat rises and remains somewhat trapped at the apex. Although the yurt is quite warm and well insulated, there are many partial thermal bridges, at the headers, the window framing and even at the roof ring and rafters. As soon as we reduced interior temperature, the cooler outside air would condense humidity on the foil, which would accrue and run down the walls or drip from points of the roof.
Using a fan at the peak of the dome ameliorated the problem, to a degree. Similarly, by adding insulation between the tarp and the exterior wall framing, we were able to reduce the temperature differential. Lastly, we recued our interior temperature by a couple of degrees and maintained that temperature day and night.
The major problem that remained was the moisture in the soil under the yurt. This spring, moisture levels have been exacerbated by heavy rainfall and a slow thaw that releases the moisture in the ice slowly.

This week, we believe we resolved that issue. By trenching around the perimeter of the yurt profile to a depth of six inches and six inches wide, we have created a mini-drainage ditch. This U-shaped trench catches the rainfall as it falls from the walls, and directs it along the perimeter of the yurt, then away. There is no opportunity for the water to pool under the yurt and contribute to the humidity issue.

Although it is early in the experiment, it seems to be working. We have experienced no condensation issues in the first three days. Yesterday, the spring rains hit again, but there is no water under the yurt, and our humidity inside the yurt is no higher than the outside. As we move through each of the initial seasons in our yurt, we have discovered new challenges and issues that would be uncommon in conventional housing. However, in spite of the spate of concerns, both of us are thrilled with this innovative living accommodation and its two overwhelming benefits: a miniscule cost (with no mortgage to pay) and its roomy in-touch-with-nature atmosphere.

Tips & Issues

▸ The design of this yurt is intended to minimize weight while maintaining strength. Consequently, the structure is very lightweight, and, if the wind is allowed to funnel beneath it, the building could act like a kite and obtain lift. The ropes that are used to secure the roof tarpaulin in place help to keep the unit anchored. However, the walls and roof assemblies are merely resting on the bottom plate, held in place only with dowels. Using metal right angle brackets (3 inches wide by 3 inches deep on each leg) and 1 ¼ inch screws for the wall chords, 2 ½ inch screws for the platform spaced at intervals on every third bottom plate, secure the wall units to the base by screwing the brackets into position on the bottom chord of the wall panel (through the tarpaulin), and into the platform base. The exterior tarpaulin skin will cover these brackets later.

▸ Wind endurance (not resistance): One of the benefits of the yurt is that it stands well against the strongest horizontal winds. For instance, our first yurt withstood gusts of 115 kph (70 mph) without so much as a shudder, yet an aspen, sixteen inches in diameter, was felled by the gusts 150 feet away.

That ability to endure the winds arises from its very design. Because it is circular, wind eddies and swirls around the building without any impediment, and the wind pressure virtually remains equal on the entire circumference. However, the drawback is that it is impossible to find a leeward side away from the wind!

Many yurt owners, though, impede this uniform air flow by building verandas or semi-closed decks on the yurt, or placing other structures too close. Not only does this put the stability of one's yurt at risk, but it decreases its low energy demands, because the wind is more able to buffet the building. If possible, keep your yurt free of extrusions such as verandas or porch entrances.

- Snow loads: One of the concerns that we had when we constructed our first yurt was that the winter snow load might be too stressful for the design if the roof. In our part of the continent, we get a fair amount of snow and lake effect snow (120 cm per winter, or 47.5 inches). While this is less than the mountainous areas or the eastern seaboard often gets, our snow stays from November until late April.

The roof trusses are designed with two-by-fours installed 24 inches on centre at the wall top plate, merging to 1.5 inches at the apex of the yurt dome. Most of the conventional, commercial yurts have a similar truss distribution, and claim that they are sufficiently solid to withstand normal snow loads. However, those manufacturers also offer wind and heavy snow load reinforcement options. Our design has an additional drawback: it is designed with a 28 degree slope, instead of the 40-45 degree slope that is needed to ensure that snow slides off the roof.

In order to distribute the weight of the snow, we installed collar ties at the seven-foot point on each truss (our yurt has a 28-foot diameter), with hurricane ties at the wall plates. To ensure lateral and diagonal stability, we used a 3/8 inch aircraft cable, adjustable through use of a turnbuckle, looped through the ends of each truss. Three by six inch reinforcing plates are affixed within two inches of the top and bottom of each joined wall section.

During the fierce winds that we encountered in late October of the first year, there was absolutely no movement of the yurt, providing us with some sense of security that the structure was sound. However, lateral wind is not comparable to vertical pressure of weight, so we have had to wait until the snow arrived to test our design.

As of January 26, we have received 10 centimetres more than the entire seasonal average of snow for our area, so measuring the impact of the snow load for a typical season is possible.

Not only has the roof assembly withstood the entire load, but it has not sagged more than 1 centimetre (1/2 inch), yet the snow depth is almost 8 inches on the lower third of the roof. To further test the strength and stability of the trusses, I climbed on the roof and put my entire weight on the mid-point between collar tie and wall plates, and collar tie and dome. No sag was noticed.

Given the additional reinforcing measures that we incorporated into the design, this durability is to be expected. However, it is welcome to see that theory and practice meet, when it comes to the strength of our design. Consequently, I have no hesitation in recommending a similar layout if you are contemplating construction of your own yurt.

▸ Opting for a more solid wall than that offered by rigid insulation alone means that you will be adding considerable weight to the structure. In one design that we built, the panels were constructed of fibreglass batt insulation sandwiched between two layers of OSB. This design was extremely strong, but each panel weighed about thirty-five pounds, compared to four pounds for each rigid insulation panel.

The rafters on this yurt were fourteen feet long, yet bore the weight of a heavy snow load without any problem.

▸ Although yurts are considerably lighter than conventional houses, there still is considerable weight to the materials, and the proper support structures need to be in place.

Many yurts are built as elevated structures, either in total or in part, since many are built in locations with considerable slopes. There is a tendency to construct these units on simple 4*4 stilts, with little regard to lateral rigidity. Additionally, when yurts are built on platforms or raised decks, they alter the wind flow in, around and under the building. This practice also exacerbates drainage and snow build-up issues, as moisture tends to flow more freely under the building.

The primary consideration should be to structural integrity. Merely walking on a platform or deck that is held up by 4*4 posts causes the building to vibrate. Like the harmonic effect of a bridge structure swaying in the wind (or a child's swing being propelled on larger and larger arcs), this rhythmic motion can increase in intensity, causing the supports to break loose over time. Cross supports should be used, in addition to ties to hold the structure caps tightly to joists or beams. Ensure that you have placed a sufficient number of stilts along the length and breadth of the platform, to prevent sag.

Wind flow can be a very serious concern for yurt design. A moderate wind, funnelled beneath the yurt, may billow, like the air beneath a parachute canopy. This air flow has a detrimental effect on heating & cooling, as well. Yurts are designed to allow for easy air flow around and over the structure, and were never designed to allow for air flow beneath.

The third concern is moisture redirection. Allowing snow load to build up under your yurt will result in high moisture content in the spring, and the contingent possible decay or mould formation on the underside of the structure. Allowing water and snow melt to drain freely under the platform, as well, will contribute to the undermining of the earthen base on which deck posts rest. This, in turn, decreases structural integrity. You should install a water redirection system on the upper edge of the yurt platform, and redirecting barriers in a lead position on each deck support leg. This will minimize the risk of water erosion.

Just because yurts are considered as an "alternative" to conventional housing does not imply that improper or inadequate construction techniques should be employed. Care in design, construction and maintenance of your yurt supporting network is a critical to building integrity as it is in conventional housing.

▸ The use of dowels in this yurt design provide both additional structural rigidity and ease of assembly. We recommend using dowels in the walls to align them to each other, in the bottom plates to provide accurate alignment and prevent shifting, in the roof rafter ring to align and secure rafters in place and in the top plates to provide structural strength, provide rigidity and assist in alignment. However, we have supplemented the dowels with strapping (the type used for shipping containers and boxes) around the perimeter of the building at the 40-42 inch height (below the windows). A third option is to use the plastic shrink wrap that is used to bundle pallets of material together. It is available in 100 or 500 yard rolls at hardware stores ($15-20). Simply wrap the first course around the building tightly and secure the first end by tucking it snugly underneath the wrap, then, stretching the material tightly, wrap around the building again.

▸ Drought brings with it the risk of fire. Because we opted to build our first yurt in an isolated, wooded location, we had no access to conventional power or water supply. Additionally, the use of polyethylene tarpaulins increased the risk of combustibility, even though the fabric had been treated with a fire retardant.
This hazard was easily dealt with by clearing away the brush and tall grasses that grew near the structure. An unintended consequence of this clearing was that small rodents were more easily deterred – a risk to the integrity of the fabric of the yurt. Larger animals, such as skunks and raccoons, now are more easily detected visually, and birds do not perch and feed so close to the yurt.
However, the greatest benefit of trimming the grass near the building (twenty feet around the perimeter) is that any grass fires can be contained more quickly and more readily. By clearing the brush back fifty feet away and the trees eighty feet, we further reduce our external fire hazard, while impacting very little on the aesthetics of the area and the wind break effect of the vegetation growth.

▸ Another problem in yurts is that of condensation, as discussed earlier. Most of the condensation in typical yurts occurs because of the low level of insulation, the trapping of heat inside the roof dome and the bridging between outside cold and inside warm air. Our original yurt was 28 feet in diameter, with a 28 degree roof pitch. It was insulated with R-6 fiberglass insulation in the wall assembly, and R-12 in the roof. Laid over this insulation, in the interior surface, is foil-coated bubble insulation, with an estimated R value of 3-5. The entire wall is sealed with foil tape, making it a vapour-proof structure. Similarly, the roof is lined with bubble insulation and taped. However, because of the joining of the roof ring and vent system, we are unable to seal the roof cavity entirely. Additionally, there is some inevitable movement of the exterior tarpaulin, which creates a convection of cool air meeting the light insulation layer.

During the daytime, sunlight on the roof often raises the temperature, during cool fall days, to a minimum of 10F above the inside temperature of the yurt. In the evening, moisture from our cooking, and moisture in the warm air (evening temperatures drop to about 30-40F lower than comfortable interior temperature) rises into the dome cavity of the yurt, and is trapped there. The vent, used to great effect in the summer, cannot be opened on cool fall or cold winter days.

As a consequence of dropping outside temperatures, the tarpaulin canvas accumulates excess condensation on the inside and outside of the fabric, which drips for hours as the air cools. The moisture in the warm interior air now conflicts with the cooler surface of the lightly insulated tarpaulin, and forms condensation which drips throughout the living space (there is nothing quite so "stimulating" as icy water dripping on you during a sound sleep!).

To resolve this problem, we have installed four 12volt min-fans near the surface of the ceiling area. Drawing less than 6 watts (at 12 volts), they run all night without a noticeable rain on our batteries, drive a small amount of the warm air at the apex of the building downward, and keep the condensation under control.

Subsequently, we have experienced only modest condensation within the yurt.

Because of the lighter insulation in the domed roof, and the fact that the heat rises and pools there when we turn off the fans, we have experienced a lot of condensation falling from the foil-backed bubble insulation that lines the inside of the roof.

Around the inside perimeter of the yurt, where walls meet the floor, moisture and some frost have accumulated. We resolved this by placing one-inch rigid foam insulation under the outer tarpaulin layer, extending it 6 inches below the wall. This provides a wind barrier, as well as insulation.

- Using exterior mirrors to gain heat: A simple idea, yet hugely effective, often is overlooked by people who assume that the best solutions are those that involve advanced technologies. This is the case with using mirrors to reflect heat and light into your yurt. When designing any building (including a yurt), one should consider the trade-off between letting in more light and heat in the winter and blocking the intense rays of the sun in the summer, Simple solutions that have proven effective include overhangs or awnings that shade the sun when it is high in the sky, but do not block that heat when winter suns rise lower on the horizon. However, proper awnings are difficult to install and incorporate into yurt structures, so an alternative is needed.

The first few months during which we lived in our yurt saw the sun burning into our south and southwest facing windows. Our only solution was to use blinds, which left the yurt darkened.

A more viable solution was a mirrored portable awning that was built into a scaffold sitting just outside the window. By putting a frame around the topside lip of the mirror, and then stapling vapour barrier to it, we were able to minimize any wind or hail damage to the mirror. In summer, the reflective side faces skyward, above the window. In fall, spring and winter, the mirror can be lowered to just below the window, with the unit sloping in toward the interior of the roof in the yurt. More, light, more heat! Total cost? Less than $20.

- Window and door installation is easier and less expensive in solid wall yurts. Because of their framing, these buildings can be constructed using standard garage windows and solid, steel insulated doors, allowing for reduced cost, energy saving and better light infiltration. It is also a lot more difficult for a raccoon to claw through a pvc & glass window than a plastic one!

- At the point where the roof rafters of a yurt meet the upright walls (particularly in a solid wall yurt design), there will be thermal bridging. This leads to condensation and cold spots in cooler months. Yurt design generally fails to compensate for this loss of heat.

In the solid wall yurt that I constructed, even though I used foil backed insulation and bubble foil insulation to minimize the extent of heat transfer, the results during a particularly cold winter were largely inadequate. However, the following year, I found the solution, and it is, in part, due to the supplementary restraint system that I incorporated in the design.

In previous discussions, I described how I had installed a dome tarpaulin that overhung the walls by about eight inches. This reduced air infiltration during wind, allowed for a greater ability to shed "horizontal" rain, protected against pest intrusion, and allowed us to create a small overhang above the windows.

I also installed another feature: ratchet strap tie downs around the upper perimeter of the walls. While the ropes that tether the roof tarpaulin to the unit generally are adequate, and the sole restraint system in many conventional designs, the ratchet straps can be adjusted around the circumference to further resist the parachute tug of high winds. At a cost of less than $40 for ninety feet of strapping, it is an inexpensive solution. That strapping also allows me to install a flexible rain gutter (see prior articles). However, its greatest benefit is in the ability that it provides to me to resolve the thermal bridging problem in the yurt.

Thermal bridging occurs, quite simply, where a harder surface that transmits hot or cold easily is exposed to the elements and to a conflicting heating or cooling source. Think of that metal counter top, and how cold it seems to the touch in winter, how hot in summer. Wood, although offering less transfer capacity, still acts as a bridge. In houses, R-factor of insulating walls is lowered, if the studs meet the outside and inside walls with no insulative materials between them. The same happens in the yurt.

To resolve the thermal dilemma, I cut pieces of two-foot wide by one inch thick rigid polystyrene insulation into five-inch lengths. Sliding these under the ratchet strapping and to the apex of the walls, all around the circumference of the yurt, I provided an R-5 insulation barrier between the top plate of the walls and rafter joints and the outside air.

Throughout the next winter (after installing the bridging insulation), I experienced no condensation in these areas, where I did so last year when the temperature neared freezing. Although an infrared thermometer shows a five-degree difference in temperatures at the bridge point versus the rest of the wall area, this differential is insignificant. Accordingly, I completed installation of similar strips of rigid insulation along the bottom perimeter of the yurt, where wall meets floor.

▶ Yurt tarp deterioration. The concept of chucking conventional housing to live in a glorified Mongolian tent – a yurt – has romantic appeal for many, aesthetic appeal for others, and eco-friendly appeal for even more. Throw in those people that eschew modern conveniences in favour of survivalist strategies and we have millions of people across North America that may embrace living in a yurt. But wait a minute! Have we considered all the cons, as well as the pros?

I have devoted the last two years to exploring the good, the bad and the ugly of yurt living, based on my own experiences. Having built a hybrid solid wall yurt in the backwoods of Manitoba, Canada, where the wind velocities often reach 100 kilometres per hour, temperatures drop to Minus 45 regularly (or climb to Plus 35C, 95F), and snowfall usurps five months of the year, I consider myself an authority on yurt living. My wife and I have loved the experience, but, in truth, there are numerous drawbacks to such a lifestyle.

One of the most recent problems has been the breakdown of the UV-protected, water repellent tarpaulins that make up the skin of the structure.

Sunlight harms every fabric. Commercial yurt makers brag of ten-year UV protection, but, most often, that is the myth rather than the reality. Farmers who "tarp" their haystacks know that most treated tarpaulins begin to show significant wear within three years. Five years is the norm for UV protection and its contingent water repellent qualities.

Yurt manufacturers recommend that pressure points on the tarpaulins be reduced, since the stretching and stress of the fabric breaks the protection down. Doubling of the tarps at specific points does, indeed, extend the usable life of the covering, but does little to extend water resistance.

Our roof tarpaulin, after only four years, requires replacement. There are a few reasons for this. First, the tarp was not properly designed. Because it was too loose in spots, wind caused segments to flutter and flap like an untethered sail. Imagine using an old fashioned wash scrub board on which you rub the tarp for hours on end, and you will have the longer-term effect of this billowing. Quickly, the fabric breaks down. Second, snow load was allowed to remain on the roof, because of its low-slope (33 degrees) design. Standing moisture caused deterioration of the moisture barrier. Lastly, the tarp was shipped with creases in it. These creases formed flaws in the continuity of the weather barrier and, here, threadbare fabric emerged within two years.

This year, we sprayed down much of the walls with water repellent spray (the same as we use on shoes, etc.). The roof tarp was treated with brush-on moisture repellent. Those areas that were treated have held, resisting this summer's rains. But it is only a matter of a couple of years before we will be replacing the entire outer skin of our yurt.

▸ A major concern of a solid wall yurt design is the added weight compared to a flexible wall system (although the proposed design has significantly reduced total structure weight. In our prototype yurt, hurricane ties were installed on the outer end of each rafter, in addition to the two screws holding the rafter ends in place. Although wind resistance is minimized with the circular design, screws are insufficient to provide the strength needed, as screws have a tendency to shear. In fact, in most jurisdictions, screws are not acceptable, according to the Building Code, for framing. Hurricane ties were also installed on the roof ring end of the rafters, as a secondary support for the six-inch bolts securing each inner rafter end.

However, in the lighter semi-solid wall design described in these plans, dowels replaced hurricane ties on the top plates and steel ties replaced hurricane ties on the rafter ring. Should you desire additional reinforcement where the top plate meets the rafter, secure the rafter using steel strapping bent to conform to the roof slope.

▸ Where the tarp skins stretch over any point, they are stressed more than when they lie flat. These critical points are at the ends of the rafters, in particular. As well, where they are secured or cut around window and door openings, they are stressed also. Most of the concern is for the UV protection they offer, as well as for premature wear. To offset these stresses, I recommend cutting a small piece of scrap tarpaulin to be placed underneath the finish layer. This double layer of fabric extends the functional life of the tarp.

Tarp that is installed too loosely will flap and flutter in the wind, which, in turn, rapidly breaks down the tarp quality. Make sure that all tarpaulin fits snugly.

- Flies: not the most attractive topic. But flies are an everyday part of our summer lives, and, in our yurt, we have discovered that flies can be particularly bothersome. The design of a yurt lends itself well to being a haven for these pests. The relatively loose fit of the tarpaulins allows these nuisances to squeeze themselves through crevices and cracks, while the permeability of the structure enables odours to waft outward. Combine these two factors with the tendency of the roof tarpaulin to trap the sun's heat, and yurts become playgrounds for flying pests.

Last autumn, for example, I removed a portion of the dome insulation to install additional snow load braces, and found hundreds of dormant flies embedded in the top side of the fibreglass insulation layer. While part of the problem may have been that the eggs pre-existed in the insulation package, recent hot days have stimulated an invasion of black and bluebottle flies.

An additional contributor to the attraction of our yurt for flying insects is the presence of our grey water tanks and compost holding tank near the home. Whenever we drain or flush these systems, flies are drawn to the site.

The round design of the yurt, as well, means that there is less air turbulence, on windy or calm and hot days. This relative tranquility allows flies to gather and reproduce.

We have implemented and tested a variety of solutions. The conventional insect trap is a general failure, for flies, mosquitoes and wasps. Unfortunately, it does a terrific job on moths, which we prefer to allow to thrive.

In desperation, we resorted to commercial chemical sprays, without success, while also flooding the environment with toxins. These sprays included perimeter, spot and space sprays, all equally ineffective.

We grow such plants as tansy, lemon balm, sorrel and other natural insect repellents. They do work, but only within a very limited and defined area. We would need to plant these sentinels every few inches around the home, and even vertically on our yurt walls to have any hope of winning the insect war.

Inside the yurt, we have resealed all of the joints of the foil-backed bubble insulation that lines our yurt roof. This action has been significantly successful, as the flies that do hatch in the domed area must migrate outward, rather than inward.

Our walls have been difficult to seal completely, given the way they moor to the roofline and floor. However, taping all of these joints has been successful, as well.

A third successful solution has been to open the dome vent while closing all but two of our windows, and using our ceiling fan to draw the air upward, instead of forcing it downward. We have installed a floor vent that allows cool air from beneath the deck to be drawn upward. This continual air movement keeps the flies from settling. The round interior of the yurt maximizes air movement, which the flies dislike.

The last proven solution that we have employed is to install a small fume hood over our cook unit, and bent it outside. With less odour to attract the flies, they now prefer to congregate near the outside vent.

We are experimenting with one other solution: mustard paste. In past years, I have had great success in deterring bugs and crawling pests in the garden, by obtaining mustard seed and wild mustard screenings from a local seed cleaner. When crushed and applied near plants, insects shy away from this hotfoot compound. We have obtained mustard oil (crushed form these same seeds), and have applied a spray under the lip of the roof tarp where it meets the wall, around the base of the wall tarp and around the window and door cutouts. So far, in the areas where this oil has been applied, there is a huge reduction in fly accumulation. However, we need to observe how long this spray lasts, and whether it has a detrimental effect on the fabric. To date, we have had to reapply the mustard paste every two to three weeks.

▸ The most common problem with yurt tarpaulins, when the yurt is built in a wooded area, is not sunlight. It is the problem of breaks, cuts and holes in the tarps caused by everything from branches breaking off nearby trees to animals and birds.

We have had squirrels puncture the roof tarp as they scamper across it, Raccoons claw gashes into the fabric as they play around and on the structure, crows pace up and down the roof with their talons pitting holes in the material, and even woodpeckers and sapsuckers try out their drumming skills on the roof.

There are a number of options for repairing these breaks in the waterproof and wind resistant shell.

Most commonly recommended is the use of tarpaulin tape. However, I find this to be the least effective, as, unless the surface is cleaned immaculately and the tape seals in the hot sun before the cool nights or moisture curl the edges, the tape lasts less than a full season.

I have used two more conventional solutions, and been satisfied with both. The first is a simple vinyl repair kit, the type used to repair pool liners, kids' air mattresses or even bicycle tire tubes. Bicycle repair kits commonly are rubber-based and less effective that vinyl or pvc compounds. The second is kitchen and bathroom silicone sealant. By applying a thick layer under the tarp hole, and then a second thin skin after the first dries, you obtain a good waterproof seal that is also flexible. Also, roofing tar works well, but is unsightly. I even tried well-chewed gum, which held up for several months.

The most environmentally friendly solution though, is also the simplest and least expensive: birch or poplar tree resin! By cutting into the tree in the spring, you can obtain a good, thick resin that will harden throughout the summer. When ready for use, simply heat the resin in a small sealed container in boiling water, then apply it in layers as it cools and hardens on the hole. Zero cost, zero impact on the environment! It is a solution appropriate for the eco-friendly yurt.

Additional Problems & General Concerns

The basic yurt design lends itself to several drawbacks.
Flexible wall yurts, for instance, have walls that are less than two inches thick. Even with the space-age bubble and foil insulation employed, you will experience more rapid heating and cooling variations inside this building. However, a solid wall yurt can be constructed of conventional studding, and insulated to higher levels using fibreglass matt insulation as well as bubble & foil or Styrofoam foil combinations. On the other hand, a yurt, because of its circular design and open concept, heats and cools much more effectively than a similarly sized bungalow. For example, our 600 square-foot yurt can be heated during minus 25 temperatures with a small radiant propane heater (4-6,000 BTUs), and a 20 pound tank will last nearly a week. A 600 square foot house would require triple that amount of fuel and still have cold and hot zones.
It is impossible to use standard glass windows in a flexible wall yurt. Consequently, the norm is to install single-sheet heavy plastic windows, which transmit a great deal of the heat or cooling between interior and exterior. A solid wall yurt, on the other hand, can accommodate standard window units (smaller sizes). Doors pose similar issues, and, more so, because most yurt vertical walls are 6'6" to 7' – less than standard door frame height.
Other infrastructure poses challenges, too. All wiring must be routed through conduit, as it is installed on the outside of the wall framing, rather than through it. An option is to use low voltage wiring and inverters throughout the building. Plumbing, too, is installed in plain view. Of course, this method of installation is much easier and quicker.
Due to the open design of these homes, privacy is impacted, and closet space is at a premium. Creative layouts can offset these concerns.

Other considerations include safe heating systems. Open flame is very risky in fabric yurts. With solid wall designs, flame retarding materials and fire-rated wall boards can be installed. Yurts may be purchased with mounting for chimney egress, but pay close attention to sparks that may burn through the roof tarpaulin! In the design plans provided herein, no allowance is made for chimney egress. It is the responsibility and liability of the owner if such amenities are implemented in the structure.

Other problems that may arise include condensation issues in cold weather, when warm, moist air rises and contacts the thinly insulated ceiling materials, condensing and falling inside the building. If tarpaulins (particularly roof tarpaulins) are not skin-tight, wind causes the tarp to billow which, in turn, packs down any matt insulation used and reduces that R-value. While the wind effect against a yurt is minimized because of the round design, this means that there are no leeward sides or areas next to the yurt, where you can huddle against the cool breeze. That also allows smoke and loose sparks to migrate around the building during the winter.

Yurts, almost always, do not meet zoning demands of any urban jurisdiction, and, therefore, do not qualify for permits. If you are building in remote locations, this will not be an issue, and some solid-wall designs, indeed, can obtain engineer certification. Proper design and construction practices should be employed regardless of whether the building meets code.

Most of us choose yurts as our living option because of its simplicity and eco-friendliness. Simplicity equates to Spartan, and Spartan means less luxury. The yurt is simple. That, in turn, should eliminate the expectation of opulence. If you want opulence, stay in the city! The yurt offers a wonderful escape and alternative to conventional housing, but be prepared for the drawbacks, as well as the advantages.

Although yurts both are vastly lighter in weight than conventional housing and offer minimal wind resistance, they, like any house, still require solid piles on which to rest.

There are a number of options available to provide a solid base for your yurt, with the simplest and most solid being beams on pad, with no posts and no piles.

When you opt to construct a solid wall yurt, rather than tarpaulin and lattice, you add significant weight to the structure, but, through the use of innovative top and bottom plates, cable reinforcement, hurricane ties and mending plates on the walls, you can build a yurt that equals any house for structural integrity.

To design a base system for a yurt by boring piles is an illustration of overkill, however. Not only do you change the definition of your building for zoning and permitting purposes, you provide a degree of reinforcement that is quite unnecessary.

The most cost effective and structurally sound combination of bases for your yurt is a simple pad system. However, you may, depending upon the grade and type of soil, need to use posts and pads, notched pads, crossties and webbing, saddle brackets and so on.

Let us look at the most simple design: beam on pad. Whereas conventional wood frame homes may require 2 by 12, 2 by 10 or doubled versions of each for beams, imbedded joists, grade beams, piles, etc., yurts, even as large as forty-two feet in diameter, will require no more than single 2 by 10 or 2 by 8 beams under 2 by 8 or 2 by 6 joists. For flat terrain with packed soil and good drainage (or in high wind regions), use a basic patio pad. For sloped ground, gravelly or soft soil or windy regions, use notched pads, or notched pads on patio pads secured with anchor bolts.

Begin by ensuring that all pads are level with each other. Simply lay the beam into or onto the pad, and then tie the joists into position, sixteen inch on centre separation. Beams should be spaced a minimum of eight feet apart, with pads spaced four feet apart for greatest stability. Reinforce the beams by nailing cross supports between beams at eight foot separation. As in conventional housing, joists should be tied together with webbing (2 by 2s).

To use post and pad on heights not exceeding twenty-four inches, use four by four double saddle brackets and double the beam using a second eighteen inch length of beam material in the upper saddle bracket. Set the foot of your four by four pile into a slotted deck pad, ensuring that the top of each four by four posts is level versus each other post top.

To use post and pad systems on heights exceeding two feet, be sure to use diagonal cross supports extending from the bottom of each post to a nearby beam or joist on two adjacent sides, alternating sides with each sequential post location.

After laying the joists into place on the beams, be sure to install appropriate headers, using a minimum of four 3.5 inch nails per joist-to-header connection, and three nails, toe-nailed into place on each beam intersection.

Since you already have ensured that the structure is level (by levelling either the pads or the tops of the posts), you should only need to check level of the joists to ensure that nothing has shifted during construction. Now, lay your underlay into place, using 2.5 inch nails. The tongue-and-grove ¾ inch OSB or plywood should be placed so that edges meet at the centre of the joist. Use plywood ties between joists for added structural strength. Your next layer of flooring will be installed at right angles to the underlay, at a later time.

Interior Accessories

The yurt, because of its open-room design, lends itself well to a variety of layout options. Below are three photos of one of our original prototype yurts, with bedroom, living room, bathroom and kitchen areas. Note the pole in one photo. This is not a support pole, but a decorative pole, intended to become a totem pole, with each visitor completing their own individual carvings on the pole.

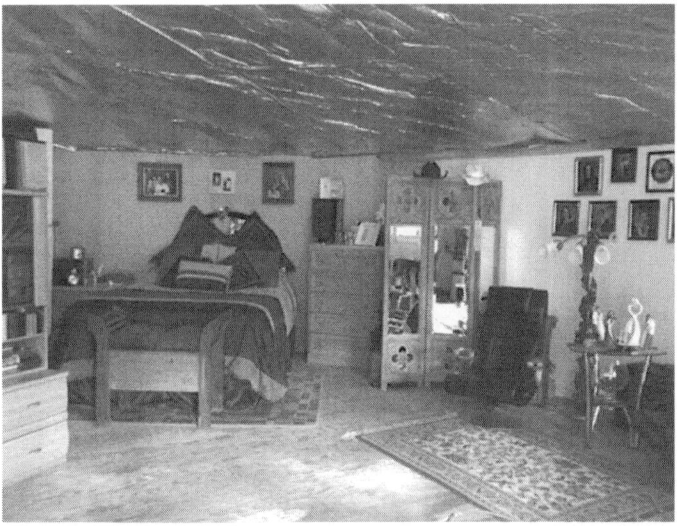

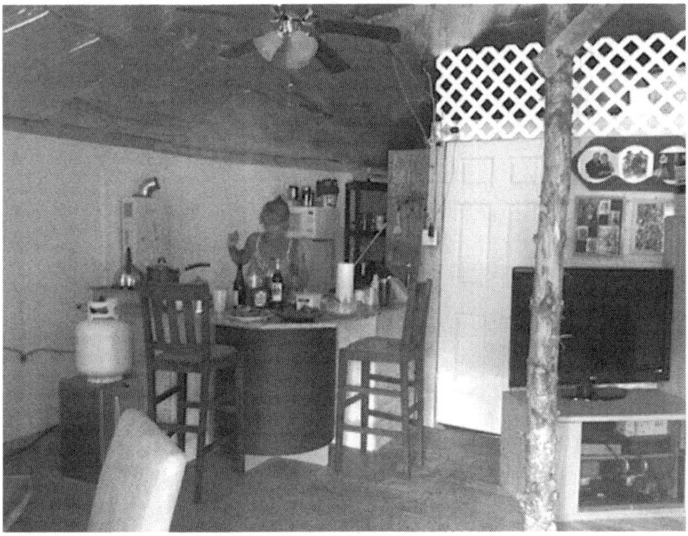

Build A Yurt Rafter Ring, Version Two

There are several designs of yurt rafter rings, each serving a particular purpose, and working best in specific environments. Snow load, wind and even humidity play a role in determining the most appropriate design. For the majority of yurt applications, the laminated design that I described in a previous article is the most effective. However, the design described in his article is suitable for smaller yurts (less than 32 feet diameter) and in low humidity locations. While it will withstand moderate snow loads, it is less structurally stable than the laminated version.

When designing a yurt roof, the same considerations that are factored into stressors on conventional housing roof rafter chords come into play. That is, you need to consider the tensions (both lateral and gravitational) on the angled chords. Truss chords endure two primary stress forces: the tendency of the bottom of the chord to push walls outward and the pull of gravity that causes slump in the riser chord. Use of collar ties works to ameliorate the gravitational warping, but, simultaneously, actually increases the stress on the top plate-to-chord heel point of contact. Fortunately, yurt roofs are so light that collar ties and webs usually are not needed.

In my prototype solid-wall yurt, I employ several redundant reinforcements for the chords. A series of mending plates, hurricane ties, aircraft cable and unique angled top plates create a structure that resists very significant outward stress. These concepts will be presented in future articles.

The rafter ring design in this article consists of two layers of ½ or 5/8 inch oriented strand board (or plywood, if OSB is unavailable) and a collage of two-by-four blocks. Other materials needed include a pound and a half of 3 ½ construction or deck screws, a pound of 1 ¾ inch construction screws, enough 3 ¼ inch framing nails to allow for four nails per block, and a quart of carpenters glue or three tubes of construction adhesive.

Begin by cutting a four by eight sheet of OSB into four-by-four pieces. Scribe a circle four feet in diameter in the first piece, and a circle three inches smaller in the second. These will form the upper and lower layers of the "sandwich" ring.

Cut as many four to six inch lengths of 2 by 4 as you will have truss chords. Lay out the pieces around the perimeter of the larger OSB circle, equidistant apart, with the pieces pointing toward the exact centre of the ring. Mark the location of each piece. Apply a layer of carpenter's glue to each piece, and re-secure them in the spots as marked. Once they have dried sufficiently, turn the assembly over and secure the pieces using two 1 ¾ inch screws per block.

Measure the distance between each block at the inner edge. Cut pieces of 2 by four that will fit accurately between each 4-6 inch piece. Do not worry too much about angling the cut edges precisely, as these pieces simply act as stabilizers for the main blocks. Apply glue to the long edges of these blocks, slide them into place between each 4-6 inch block and secure them using 3 ¼ inch screws, toenail angled into place. Use one nail per longer block to nail the spacers into place.

Turn the assembly over again, apply glue to the exposed edge of all of the blocks, and attach the second ring, with its centre aligning exactly with the centre of the larger ring. Use two screws per block, as in the prior side of the sandwich. Turn the assembly over once again, and screw in two screws per spacer block.

This rafter ring is much lighter than the laminated version described in prior articles, and is much easier to raise into place. With the smaller ring on the lower side of this sandwich design, the truss chords, once cut on the proper angle, will slide into the notches quite easily and will hold themselves in place as each truss in installed. However, the drawback to this design is the tendency for the OSB to expand and weaken if it gets wet, or for the screws to pull through if they are set too deep in the OSB.

Disclaimer: engineers, permits, fire safety

These plans are guidelines only. The quality of the product is your responsibility, and we make no claims as to the integrity and safety of the design. This product does not bear an architect's or engineer's endorsement, and it is the responsibility of the builder to ensure compliance with all building code, fire code, plumbing and electrical installation requirements.
The fabric and insulation used in this design does not meet the fire rating (retardant, smoke) standards for most construction requirements, and should not be considered to be a permanent structure (either residence or outbuilding).
The builder/owner is responsible to ensure that all required permits and permissions are obtained by the owner.

Our first series of yurts exposed problems and benefits that are not discussed in most literature regarding these structures. Design issues, weather, wildlife problems and so on all provided challenges. Yet, with all these inconveniences, the yurt life is the life for me! No mortgage, little cost, freedom, solitude, and the feeling that we are denting our environment only minimally, all are uplifting elements. So, problems have happened, but they are far, far less than the benefits. We hope that you, too, enjoy your yurt!

Visit www.robertflee.com for links to several blogs related to yurt living, including http://movingtoayurt.blogspot.com and http://eatingwild.blogspot.com. You may also be interested in our blogs on living a simple life, including http://findingtheoasis.blogspot.com and http://leanandgreenliving.blogspot.com. Questions or comments? Email me at admin@robertflee.com.

Printed in Great Britain
by Amazon.co.uk, Ltd.,
Marston Gate.